EDITOR: Maryanne Blacker

FOOD EDITOR: Pamela Clark

• • •

DESIGNER: Neil Carlyle

ARTISTS: Felicity Edmonds, Helen Forrest

• • •

DEPUTY FOOD EDITORS:
Jan Castorina, Karen Green

ASSOCIATE FOOD EDITOR: Enid Morrison

CHIEF HOME ECONOMIST: Kathy Wharton

DEPUTY CHIEF HOME ECONOMIST:
Louise Patniotis

HOME ECONOMISTS: Tracey Kern, Quinton Kohler,
Jill Lange, Alexandra McCowan, Kathy McGarry,
Kathy Snowball, Dimitra Stais

EDITORIAL COORDINATOR: Elizabeth Hooper

KITCHEN ASSISTANT: Amy Wong

• • •

STYLISTS: Marie-Helene Clauzon, Rosemary de Santis,
Carolyn Fienberg, Michelle Gorry, Jacqui Hing

PHOTOGRAPHERS: Bruce Allan, Kevin Brown,
Robert Clark, Robert Taylor, Jon Waddy

• • •

HOME LIBRARY STAFF:

ASSISTANT EDITOR: Beverley Hudec

DESIGNER: Paula Wooller

EDITORIAL COORDINATOR: Fiona Nicholas

• • •

ACP PUBLISHER: Richard Walsh

ACP ASSOCIATE PUBLISHER: Bob Neil

• • •

Produced by The Australian Women's Weekly Home Library.
Typeset by ACP Colour Graphics Pty Ltd. Printed by Dai
Nippon Co., Ltd in Japan.
Published by ACP Publishing Pty Ltd, 54 Park Street, Sydney.
♦ AUSTRALIA: Distributed by Network Distribution Company,
54 Park Street Sydney, (02) 282 8777.
♦ UNITED KINGDOM: Distributed in the U.K. by Australian
Consolidated Press (UK) Ltd, 20 Galowhill Rd, Brackmills,
Northampton NN4 OEE (0604) 760 456.
♦ CANADA: Distributed in Canada by Whitecap
Books Ltd, 1086 West 3rd St,
North Vancouver V7P 3J6 (604) 980 9852.
♦ NEW ZEALAND: Distributed in New Zealand by Netlink
Distribution Company, 17B Hargreaves St, Level 5,
College Hill, Auckland 1 (9) 302 7616.
♦ SOUTH AFRICA: Distributed in South Africa by Intermag,
PO Box 57394, Springfield 2137 (011) 493 3200.
ACN 053 273 546.

• • •

Easy Thai-style Cookery

Includes index.
ISBN 0 949128 33 3.

1. Cookery, Thai. (Series: Australian
Women's Weekly Home Library).

641.59593

• • •

We would like to thank the Natural Gas Company and Rinnai
for their help with this book.

COVER: Prawn Curry with Fresh Pineapple and
Asparagus, page 46.
Bowl: Corso de Fiori; statuette,cloth: Private Life
OPPOSITE: Chicken and Noodle Soup, page 20.
BACK COVER: Mixed Satay, page 4.

W9-BFE-348

Easy Thai-style Cookery

The delicate flavours of Thai cuisine that have captivated the
Australian palate in a big way are not difficult to re-create in
your own kitchen. We show you how, in easy-to-follow
step-by-step photographs. These 82 recipes have been modified
and simplified – we don't claim they are true-blue Thai –
but it is important to use the ingredients specified, such as
coriander, fish sauce and galangal, which you will be able to
find in most Asian food shops and some specialty shops and
delicatessens. And when you're serving, why not do it the Thai
way: serve soups, salads and main courses all at the same
time with freshly boiled plain rice. And, eat the meal with a
fork and spoon, not chopsticks.

Pamela Clark

FOOD EDITOR

BRITISH & NORTH AMERICAN READERS: Please note that Australian
cup and spoon measurements are metric. A Quick Conversion Guide
appears on page 128.
A glossary explaining unfamiliar terms and ingredients appears on page 124.

Entrees

Serving entrees just before the main course, as in Western meals, is virtually unknown in Thai households. Instead, entrees are sometimes served to guests before they sit down at the dinner table. Snacks are also served throughout the day, and at parties and celebrations. Several of our entrees can easily be modified into main courses using a dash of flexibility and imagination.

BEEF AND PRAWN POUCHES

2 tablespoons oil
1 clove garlic, crushed
1 small onion, finely chopped
2 teaspoons chopped fresh ginger
80g minced beef
60g cooked small prawns, shelled
1 small carrot, grated
2 green shallots, chopped
1 tablespoon chopped fresh basil
1 tablespoon sugar
250g packet gow gees pastry
1 egg, lightly beaten
oil for deep-frying
1 medium fresh red chilli, sliced

SWEET CHILLI SAUCE
½ cup water
¼ cup white vinegar
1 teaspoon hoi sin sauce
1 small fresh red chilli, chopped
½ cup brown sugar, firmly packed

■ Can be prepared 3 hours ahead.
■ Storage: Covered, in refrigerator.
■ Freeze: Uncooked pouches suitable.
■ Microwave: Not suitable.

Makes about 30.

1: Heat oil in pan, add garlic, cook, stirring, until lightly browned. Add onion and ginger, cook, stirring, 1 minute. Add mince, cook, stirring, until mince is well browned. Stir in prawns, carrot and shallots, cook 1 minute; cool. Stir in basil and sugar.

2: Brush pastry sheets with egg, top with level teaspoons of mince mixture. Pull up edges of pastry around mixture, pinch together to seal.

3: Just before serving, deep-fry pouches in hot oil, in batches, until well browned; drain on absorbent paper. Serve pouches hot with hot sweet chilli sauce; top with sliced chilli.

Sweet Chilli Sauce: Combine all ingredients in pan, stir over heat until sugar is dissolved. Bring to boil, simmer, uncovered, for about 5 minutes or until slightly thickened.

MIXED SATAY

250g chicken breast fillets, sliced
250g piece beef eye fillet, sliced
250g pork fillets, sliced
2 cloves garlic, crushed
½ teaspoon ground coriander
¼ teaspoon ground cumin
½ teaspoon curry powder
2 tablespoons oil
1 tablespoon brown sugar
1 tablespoon fish sauce
¼ teaspoon sambal oelek

SATAY SAUCE
1 cup (120g) peanuts
1 tablespoon oil
1 onion, finely chopped
2 cloves garlic, crushed
2 medium fresh red chillies,
    finely chopped
1 tablespoon finely chopped fresh
    lemon grass
½ teaspoon curry powder
¼ teaspoon ground cumin
¼ teaspoon chopped
    fresh coriander root
1 cup coconut milk
2 tablespoons brown sugar
2 teaspoons tamarind sauce
2 teaspoons lime juice

SWEET AND SOUR SAUCE
¼ cup white vinegar
½ cup sugar
1½ tablespoons water
½ carrot, finely chopped
¼ small green cucumber,
    seeded, chopped

■ Satay skewers can be prepared a day
    ahead; sauces made 6 hours ahead.
■ Storage: Satay skewers, covered, in
    refrigerator. Sauces, covered, at room
    temperature.
■ Freeze: Uncooked skewers suitable.
■ Microwave: Not suitable.

Makes 30.

1: Thread chicken, beef and pork onto skewers, place in shallow dish. Combine garlic, coriander, cumin, curry powder, oil, sugar, sauce and sambal oelek in bowl; pour over skewers. Cover, refrigerate skewers for at least 1 hour.

2: Grill skewers until tender, turning often; serve with sauces.

3: Satay Sauce: Blend or process nuts until crushed. Heat oil in wok, add onion, garlic, chillies, lemon grass, curry powder, cumin and coriander root, cook, stirring, until onion is soft. Add nuts and remaining ingredients, stir until heated through.

4: Sweet and Sour Sauce: Combine vinegar, sugar and water in pan, stir until sugar is dissolved, bring to boil. Boil, uncovered, for 3 minutes. Pour syrup over carrot and cucumber in serving bowl; cool.

PEANUT CURRY WITH EGGS

2 tablespoons red curry paste
½ teaspoon canned drained
   green peppercorns
¼ teaspoon ground cardamom
2 teaspoons paprika
2½ cups coconut milk
½ teaspoon palm sugar
2 tablespoons fish sauce
250g frozen peas, thawed
8 hard-boiled eggs, halved
½ cup coarsely chopped peanuts

■ Curry paste mixture can be prepared
  a week ahead.
■ Storage: Covered, in refrigerator.
■ Freeze: Not suitable.
■ Microwave: Suitable.

Serves 6.

*Fabric from Gallery Nomad. Accessories from Java
Bazaar. Bowl from Morgan Imports*

1: Combine paste, peppercorns and spices in pan. Add ½ cup of the coconut milk to the curry paste mixture, cook 1 minute or until fragrant.

2: Just before serving, combine remaining coconut milk, sugar, sauce, peas and curry mixture in pan, stir until heated through; pour curry around eggs, sprinkle with peanuts.

CORN AND CHICKEN FRITTERS

2 eggs, lightly beaten
2 x 440g cans corn kernels, drained
2 tablespoons cornflour
250g chicken breast fillets, chopped
2 teaspoons chopped fresh coriander
1 teaspoon sugar
1 tablespoon light soy sauce
2 tablespoons oil

■ Batter can be prepared 3 hours ahead.
■ Storage: Covered, in refrigerator.
■ Freeze: Not suitable.
■ Microwave: Not suitable.

Makes about 40.

1: Combine eggs, corn, cornflour, chicken, coriander, sugar and sauce in bowl; mix well.

2: Just before serving, heat oil in pan, drop level tablespoons of corn mixture into pan, cook on both sides until well browned and cooked; drain on absorbent paper.

SPRING ROLLS WITH CHILLI AND PEANUT SAUCE

50g rice vermicelli
250g lean pork
1 tablespoon oil
1 clove garlic, crushed
1 teaspoon chopped fresh red chillies
2 green shallots, chopped
1 carrot, grated
1 tablespoon chopped fresh
    coriander root
1 tablespoon chopped fresh
    coriander leaves
1 teaspoon fish sauce
100g cooked prawns, shelled,
    chopped
30 spring roll pastry sheets
1 tablespoon cornflour
2 tablespoons water
oil for deep-frying

CHILLI AND PEANUT SAUCE
¼ cup white vinegar
2 tablespoons sugar
½ small green cucumber, peeled,
    seeded, chopped
¼ teaspoon chopped fresh red chilli
1 tablespoon chopped peanuts

■ Rolls can be prepared 3 hours ahead.
■ Storage: Covered, in refrigerator.
■ Freeze: Not suitable.
■ Microwave: Not suitable.

Makes 30.

1: Cover vermicelli with warm water in bowl, stand 10 minutes; drain well.

2: Process pork until finely minced. Heat oil in pan, add pork, garlic and chillies, cook, stirring, until pork is browned. Add shallots, carrot, coriander root and leaves, sauce, prawns and vermicelli. Cook, stirring, until heated through; cool.

3: Place level tablespoons of mixture on a corner of each pastry sheet, brush edges with blended cornflour and water. Fold left and right corners inwards, then bottom corner inwards. Roll pastry sheet to enclose filling.

4: Just before serving, deep-fry rolls in hot oil until well browned; drain on absorbent paper. Serve hot spring rolls with chilli and peanut sauce.

5: Chilli and Peanut Sauce: Combine vinegar and sugar in pan, stir over heat until sugar is dissolved. Bring to boil, simmer, uncovered, for about 4 minutes or until syrup just begins to colour. Remove syrup from heat, transfer to bowl; cool slightly. Stir in remaining ingredients.

RED CURRY FISH CAKES

1kg redfish fillets
1 egg
2 tablespoons chopped
    fresh coriander
2 teaspoons sugar
100g green beans, thinly sliced
oil for deep-frying

RED CURRY PASTE
1 small red Spanish onion, chopped
3 cloves garlic, crushed
2 tablespoons chopped fresh
    lemon grass
3 teaspoons chopped fresh
    coriander root
2 teaspoons dried chilli flakes
1 teaspoon galangal powder
1 teaspoon grated lime rind
½ teaspoon shrimp paste
1 dried kaffir lime leaf
3 teaspoons paprika
½ teaspoon turmeric
½ teaspoon cumin seeds
3 teaspoons oil

■ Fish cakes can be prepared a day
  ahead. Red curry paste can be made
  a week ahead.
■ Storage: Covered, in refrigerator.
■ Freeze: Uncooked fish cakes suitable.
■ Microwave: Not suitable.

Makes about 25.

1: Blend or process fish, egg, coriander, sugar and ⅓ cup of red curry paste until well combined and smooth.

2: Combine fish mixture and beans in bowl; mix well.

3: Roll 2 level tablespoons of mixture into a ball, flatten slightly; repeat with remaining mixture.

4: Just before serving, deep-fry fish cakes in hot oil until well browned and cooked; drain on absorbent paper.

5: Curry Paste: Blend or process all ingredients until smooth.

CRISPY EGGS WITH PORK AND PRAWN

8 hard-boiled eggs
200g cooked prawns, shelled, finely
    chopped
200g minced pork
2 tablespoons coconut cream
2 tablespoons chopped fresh
    coriander
1 tablespoon fish sauce
oil for deep-frying

BATTER
½ cup plain flour
½ cup self-raising flour
1 teaspoon sugar
2 tablespoons oil
1 cup water

■ Eggs can be prepared a day ahead.
■ Storage: Covered, in refrigerator.
■ Freeze: Not suitable.
■ Microwave: Not suitable.

Makes 16.

1: Cut eggs in half, remove yolks. Mash egg yolks in bowl with fork, add prawns, pork, coconut cream, coriander and sauce; mix well. Divide pork mixture into 16 portions. Shape portions over egg white halves to form egg shapes; cover, refrigerate 1 hour.

2: Just before serving, dip egg halves into batter, deep-fry in hot oil until browned and cooked through; drain on absorbent paper. Serve hot.

3: Batter: Sift flours and sugar into bowl, gradually stir in oil and water, beat to a smooth batter (or blend or process ingredients until smooth); cover, stand 20 minutes.

China from Limoges

Soups

Soups are usually served as part of the main Thai meal and can be eaten separately or spooned onto your plate and eaten with rice. Clear hot and sour Thai soups are memorable for their subtle yet bold combination of flavours using lemon grass, lemon juice and chilli. We've also included some richer soups using noodles and coconut milk.

PUMPKIN AND COCONUT CREAM SOUP

1 tablespoon oil
1 clove garlic, crushed
4 green shallots, chopped
2 small fresh red chillies, chopped
1 tablespoon chopped fresh
   lemon grass
½ teaspoon shrimp paste
2 small chicken stock cubes,
   crumbled
2 cups boiling water
500g pumpkin, chopped
400ml can coconut cream
250g cooked small prawns,
   shelled
1 tablespoon shredded fresh basil

■ Soup can be made a day ahead.
■ Storage: Covered, in refrigerator.
■ Freeze: Not suitable.
■ Microwave: Suitable.

Serves 4.

1: Heat oil in pan, add garlic, shallots, chillies, lemon grass and paste, cook, stirring, until shallots are soft.

3: Add prawns, stir until heated through. Serve soup sprinkled with basil.

2: Add stock cubes and water, bring to boil, add pumpkin, simmer, covered, for 10 minutes. Stir in coconut cream, simmer, covered, for 5 minutes or until pumpkin is tender.

Bowl from Accoutrement

CHICKEN AND COCONUT MILK SOUP

500g chicken breast fillets
1¼ litres (5 cups) coconut milk
5 dried kaffir lime leaves
4 pieces dried galangal
1 stem fresh lemon grass, sliced
2 tablespoons lemon juice
½ teaspoon sugar
2 tablespoons fish sauce
2 teaspoons chopped fresh
   red chillies
5 green shallots, shredded
fresh coriander leaves

■ Best made just before serving.
■ Freeze: Not suitable.
■ Microwave: Suitable.

Serves 4.

1: Cut chicken into 1cm strips.

2: Combine coconut milk, leaves, galangal and lemon grass in pan, bring to boil. Add chicken, simmer, uncovered, until chicken is tender.

3: Stir in juice, sugar, sauce, chillies and shallots, bring to boil, simmer, uncovered, for 3 minutes. Serve soup sprinkled with coriander leaves.

Fabric from Accoutrement

HOT AND SOUR PRAWN SOUP

500g uncooked prawns
2 small fresh red chillies, chopped
1 tablespoon sliced fresh
   lemon grass
1 teaspoon grated fresh ginger
2 teaspoons fish sauce
2 teaspoons light soy sauce
1 tablespoon lime juice
2 teaspoons sugar
4 green shallots, chopped
425g can whole straw mushrooms,
   rinsed, drained

FISH STOCK
500g white fish bones
2½ litres (10 cups) water
2 stems fresh lemon grass, chopped
1 small fresh red chilli, halved
4 dried kaffir lime leaves
3 pieces dried galangal

■ Stock best made a day ahead.
■ Storage: Covered, in refrigerator.
■ Freeze: Stock suitable.
■ Microwave: Suitable.

Serves 4.

1: Shell prawns leaving tails intact. Measure 6 cups of the stock into pan, leaving sediment in pan.

2: Add prawns, chillies, lemon grass, ginger, sauces, juice, sugar, shallots and mushrooms. Bring to boil, simmer, uncovered, until prawns are tender.

3: Fish Stock: Combine all ingredients in pan, bring to boil, simmer, covered, for 20 minutes. Strain stock through fine strainer; cover, refrigerate overnight.

Bowl from Noritake

MIXED SEAFOOD SOUP

250g uncooked king prawns
6 (about 500g) baby octopus
2 litres (8 cups) water
2 tablespoons oil
1 small onion, finely chopped
3 teaspoons grated fresh ginger
3 cloves garlic, crushed
1 stem fresh lemon grass,
**   finely chopped**
pinch saffron
1 fresh coriander root,
**   finely chopped**
1 teaspoon sweet chilli sauce
1½ tablespoons fish sauce
⅓ cup lime juice
4 dried kaffir lime leaves
½ teaspoon cumin seeds
400ml can coconut cream
1 tablespoon raw sugar
160g scallops
250g white fish fillets, chopped
fresh coriander leaves

■ Recipe can be prepared a day ahead.
■ Storage: Covered, in refrigerator.
■ Freeze: Not suitable.
■ Microwave: Suitable.

Serves 6.

1: Shell prawns, reserve heads. Remove heads and beaks from octopus, cut tentacles into pairs.

2: Combine reserved prawn heads with water in pan, slowly bring to boil, simmer, uncovered, for 30 minutes. Cool stock, strain; reserve stock.

3: Heat oil in pan, add onion, ginger, garlic, lemon grass, saffron, coriander root and sauces, cook, stirring, until onion is soft.

4: Add reserved stock, juice, lime leaves and seeds, bring to boil, simmer, uncovered, for 15 minutes. Stir in coconut cream and sugar, simmer 5 minutes.

5: Just before serving, stir in seafood, simmer for about 2 minutes or until seafood is tender. Sprinkle with coriander.

CHICKEN AND NOODLE SOUP

400g chicken breast fillets
2 cloves garlic, crushed
3 teaspoons ground cumin
½ teaspoon turmeric
1½ litres (6 cups) water
2 teaspoons chicken stock powder
1 tablespoon sugar
½ teaspoon shrimp paste
3 teaspoons sambal oelek
1 piece dried galangal
50g rice vermicelli
1 cup (75g) bean sprouts
3 lettuce leaves, shredded
2 tablespoons chopped
 fresh coriander

■ Soup can be prepared a day ahead.
■ Storage: Covered, in refrigerator.
■ Freeze: Not suitable.
■ Microwave: Suitable.

Serves 6.

1: Cut chicken into 2cm slices. Combine garlic, cumin and turmeric in pan, stir over heat for about 1 minute or until fragrant.

2: Add chicken, water, stock powder, sugar, paste, sambal oelek and galangal to pan, stir until combined. Bring to boil, simmer, uncovered, for 10 minutes.

3: Add vermicelli to pan, simmer for 10 minutes.

4: Just before serving, stir in bean sprouts, lettuce and coriander.

Accessories from Java Bazaar

SPICY BEEF SOUP

375g round steak, thinly sliced
1 tablespoon dry red wine
1½ litres (6 cups) water
2 small beef stock cubes,
    crumbled
6 green shallots, chopped
2 cloves garlic, sliced
3 fresh coriander roots
2 tablespoons dark soy sauce
2 teaspoons brown sugar
1 small fresh red chilli,
    finely chopped
425g can straw mushrooms, drained
¼ cup lime juice
1 tablespoon chopped fresh
    coriander leaves

■ Recipe can be prepared a day ahead.
■ Storage: Covered, in refrigerator.
■ Freeze: Not suitable.
■ Microwave: Suitable.

Serves 6.

1: Combine steak and wine in bowl; cover, stand 15 minutes.

2: Combine water, stock cubes, shallots, garlic, coriander roots, sauce, sugar and half the chilli in pan. Bring to boil, simmer, uncovered, for 15 minutes. Drain mixture, return liquid to pan, discard pulp.

3: Just before serving, bring stock to boil, add steak, mushrooms, remaining chilli and juice, simmer, uncovered, until heated through. Stir in coriander leaves.

Salads

Vegetables are generally eaten raw, dipped in sauces, served over a bed of lettuce and garnished with coriander leaves. They are also stir-fried or lightly steamed, and sometimes, small amounts of fish, minced meat or chicken are added as a flavour contrast. Our recipes can be served as accompaniments to a main meal or simply as a light meal.

STIR-FRIED SWEET AND SOUR VEGETABLES

2 cloves garlic
2 small fresh red chillies
500g fresh asparagus
2 long green cucumbers
1 tablespoon oil
100g snow peas
250g broccoli flowerets
1 green pepper, chopped
2 tablespoons fish sauce
1½ tablespoons white vinegar
1 tablespoon sugar

■ Best made close to serving.
■ Freeze: Not suitable.
■ Microwave: Suitable.

Serves 6.

1: Cut garlic and chillies into long, thin strips. Cut asparagus into 5cm lengths; cut cucumbers in half lengthways, remove seeds, then slice cucumbers thickly.

2: Heat oil in wok, add garlic and chillies, stir-fry until lightly browned; remove from wok; leave oil in wok.

3: Reheat wok, add vegetables, stir-fry until vegetables are just tender.

4: Add combined sauce, vinegar and sugar, stir-fry 1 minute. Serve vegetables sprinkled with garlic and chillies.

Gold accessories from Morgan Imports

SPICY TOFU SALAD

750g tofu, drained
1 small red Spanish onion
1 carrot
1 green pepper
2 tablespoons peanuts, chopped
DRESSING
2 small fresh red chillies,
**   finely chopped**
¼ cup lime juice
2 tablespoons brown sugar
1 tablespoon fish sauce
1 stem fresh lemon grass,
**   thinly sliced**

■ Salad can be made 3 hours ahead.
■ Storage: Covered, in refrigerator.
■ Freeze: Not suitable.
■ Microwave: Not suitable.

Serves 6.

1: Cut tofu into 1cm cubes. Cut onion in half, cut into thin slices. Cut carrot and pepper into thin strips.

2: Combine tofu, onion, carrot, pepper and dressing in bowl; mix well. Cover, refrigerate 3 hours. Serve salad sprinkled with peanuts.

3: Dressing: Combine chillies, juice, sugar, sauce and lemon grass in jar; shake well.

Left: Dishes from Accoutrement

BEANS WITH GINGER AND COCONUT MILK

500g green beans
1 tablespoon oil
2 stems fresh lemon grass,
**   finely chopped**
2 tablespoons grated fresh ginger
1 small fresh red chilli, chopped
1 cup coconut milk
4 cups (about 350g) shredded
**   cabbage**

■ Best made just before serving.
■ Freeze: Not suitable.
■ Microwave: Not suitable.

Serves 6.

1: Cut beans into 5cm lengths. Heat oil in wok, add lemon grass, ginger and chilli, cook until oil begins to bubble.

2: Stir in coconut milk and beans, bring to boil, simmer, uncovered, for about 3 minutes or until beans are just tender. Serve bean mixture over cabbage.

CABBAGE SALAD WITH LIME JUICE DRESSING

3 large fresh red chillies
2 tablespoons oil
6 cloves garlic, sliced
6 green shallots, sliced
½ cabbage, shredded
1 tablespoon crushed peanuts

DRESSING
2 tablespoons fish sauce
2 tablespoons lime juice
½ cup coconut milk

■ Salad can be made a day ahead.
■ Storage: Covered, in refrigerator.
■ Freeze: Not suitable.
■ Microwave: Not suitable.

Serves 6.

1: Cut chillies into thin strips. Heat oil in pan, stir-fry chillies, garlic and shallots separately until lightly browned and crisp; drain on absorbent paper.

2: Add cabbage to pan of boiling water, drain immediately.

3: Combine cabbage and dressing in bowl, mix well. Serve salad topped with stir-fried chilli mixture and nuts.

4: Dressing: Combine all ingredients in bowl; mix well.

FRUIT SALAD WITH SAVOURY COCONUT DRESSING

1 apple
1 banana
½ red papaw
1 cup coconut milk
1 small fresh red chilli, chopped
1 tablespoon chopped fresh coriander
2 tablespoons lime juice
1 tablespoon fish sauce
¼ cup peanuts
6 cos lettuce leaves

■ Salad best made 1 hour ahead.
■ Storage: Covered, in refrigerator.
■ Freeze: Not suitable.

Serves 4.

1: Cut apple in half, remove core, cut apple into thin slices, slice banana, chop papaw. Combine coconut milk, chilli, coriander, juice and sauce in bowl.

2: Combine fruit and nuts in bowl with coconut milk dressing, mix well; cover, refrigerate 1 hour before serving. Serve over lettuce.

SWEET AND SOUR TOFU

375g tofu, drained
¼ cup oil
1 clove garlic, sliced
200g green beans, sliced
1 onion, sliced
1 carrot, sliced
200g broccoli, chopped
1 stick celery, sliced
2 green shallots, chopped
1 tablespoon tamarind sauce
1 tablespoon fish sauce
2 tablespoons oyster sauce
1 tablespoon light soy sauce
1 tablespoon sweet chilli sauce
1 tablespoon tomato paste
2 tablespoons sugar
1 tablespoon white vinegar
¼ teaspoon ground star anise
1 teaspoon cornflour
1 cup water

■ Best made just before serving.
■ Freeze: Not suitable.
■ Microwave: Not suitable.

Serves 6.

1: Cut tofu into 1½cm cubes.

2: Heat oil in wok, add garlic, cook 30 seconds, remove and discard garlic. Add tofu to wok in batches, stir-fry gently until lightly browned; remove from wok.

3: Add beans, onion and carrot, stir-fry until vegetables are almost tender. Add broccoli, celery and shallots, sauces, paste, sugar, vinegar and spice, stir-fry 2 minutes. Stir in tofu with blended cornflour and water; stir-fry gently until sauce boils and thickens slightly.

TOFU AND EGG SALAD

2 teaspoons chopped fresh
    coriander root
1 clove garlic, crushed
1 tablespoon grated fresh ginger
2 tablespoons brown sugar
2 tablespoons dark soy sauce
1 teaspoon five spice powder
2 teaspoons oil
¼ cup water
6 (about 200g) radishes
375g tofu, drained, cubed
1 tablespoon chopped fresh
    coriander leaves
1 small fresh red chilli, finely chopped
1 hard-boiled egg, chopped

■ Can be prepared 6 hours ahead.
■ Storage: Covered, in refrigerator.
■ Freeze: Not suitable.
■ Microwave: Not suitable.

Serves 4.

1: Blend coriander root, garlic, ginger, sugar, sauce and five spice powder until well combined.

2: Heat oil in pan, add blended mixture, cook, stirring, for about 2 minutes or until fragrant. Stir in water; cool to room temperature.

3: Cut radishes into thin strips. Combine tofu and radish in bowl, pour over blended mixture, cover, stand for 2 hours, stirring occasionally.

4: Just before serving, drain tofu mixture, combine with coriander leaves, chilli and egg.

MIXED VEGETABLES WITH MUSHROOMS

1 small zucchini
1 medium carrot
2 tablespoons oil
3 small fresh red chillies, finely
    chopped
1 stem fresh lemon grass,
    finely chopped
½ cup coconut milk
1 dried kaffir lime leaf
100g green beans, sliced
1 small red pepper, sliced
150g broccoli, chopped
425g can straw mushrooms, drained
1 tablespoon chopped fresh basil
1 bunch Chinese broccoli, shredded

■ Best made just before serving.
■ Freeze: Not suitable.
■ Microwave: Not suitable.

Serves 4.

1: Cut zucchini and carrot into thin strips. Heat oil in wok, add chillies and lemon grass, cook, stirring, for about 2 minutes or until fragrant. Add coconut milk and lime leaf, stir until combined and mixture is heated through.

2: Add beans, pepper, zucchini, carrot and broccoli, stir-fry until vegetables are just tender. Add straw mushrooms and basil, stir-fry until heated through.

3: Steam or microwave Chinese broccoli until just tender, serve tossed with mixed vegetables.

Left: Plate from Accoutrement. Box and fabric from Gallery Nomad

WATER CHESTNUT SALAD
WITH FILLET OF PORK

1 tablespoon oil
250g pork fillet
8 green shallots
3 cloves garlic, sliced
1 tablespoon fish sauce
2 tablespoons lemon juice
3 teaspoons sugar
8 (165g) medium cooked
   prawns, shelled
50g crab meat, flaked
230g can water chestnuts, drained
1 tablespoon chopped fresh coriander

■ Pork can be prepared a day ahead,
   shallot mixture several hours ahead.
■ Storage: Covered, in refrigerator.
■ Freeze: Not suitable.
■ Microwave: Suitable.

Serves 4.

1: Heat oil in pan, add pork, cook, turning frequently, until well browned and tender. Remove pork from pan, drain, cool. Cut into 1cm slices, then cut into halves.

2: Cut shallots into 6cm strips. Reheat pan, add garlic and shallots, stir-fry for 1 minute; add sauce, juice and sugar, stir-fry until heated through; cool.

3: Just before serving, combine pork, shallot mixture, prawns, crab and water chestnuts in bowl, sprinkle with coriander.

Left: Fabric from Gallery Nomad. Bowl from Morgan Imports

STIR-FRIED VEGETABLES WITH CRACKED BLACK PEPPER

1 bunch bok choy
2 tablespoons oil
2 cloves garlic, crushed
3 carrots (350g), sliced
250g beans, halved
1 cup (100g) bean sprouts,
    firmly packed
¼ cup water
1 tablespoon fish sauce
1 tablespoon oyster sauce
1 teaspoon sugar
1 teaspoon cracked black
    peppercorns

■ Best made just before serving.
■ Freeze: Not suitable.
■ Microwave: Suitable.

Serves 4.

1: Tear bok choy into large pieces. Heat oil in wok, add garlic, carrots and beans, stir-fry until vegetables are almost tender.

2: Stir in bok choy leaves, sprouts, water, sauces, sugar and peppercorns, bring to boil, simmer, uncovered, until vegetables are as tender as desired.

DEEP-FRIED TOFU WITH PEANUT SAUCE

2 x 297g packets tofu, drained
oil for deep-frying

PEANUT SAUCE
1 fresh coriander root, finely chopped
1 small fresh red chilli, finely chopped
2 cloves garlic, crushed
1 tablespoon sugar
2 tablespoons rice vinegar
⅓ cup smooth peanut butter
¼ cup coconut milk

■ Sauce can be made 3 days ahead.
■ Storage: Covered, in refrigerator.
■ Freeze: Not suitable.
■ Microwave: Sauce suitable.

Serves 6.

1: Wrap tofu in 3 sheets of absorbent paper, weigh down with plate; stand 4 hours.

2: Just before serving, cut tofu into 2cm cubes. Deep-fry cubes in hot oil in batches until well browned; drain on absorbent paper. Serve hot with warm peanut sauce.

3: Peanut Sauce: Combine coriander root, chilli, garlic, sugar and vinegar in pan, stir over heat until sugar is dissolved. Stir in peanut butter and coconut milk, stir until heated through. Serve sprinkled with fresh coriander and chilli, if desired.

Plates from Limoges

EGGPLANT AND DRIED SHRIMP SALAD

2 medium (about 900g) eggplants
2 teaspoons chopped fresh
    coriander root
1 teaspoon cracked black
    peppercorns
3 cloves garlic, crushed
1 teaspoon sugar
2 tablespoons fish sauce
1 medium fresh red chilli, chopped
2 tablespoons oil
¼ cup lime juice
⅓ cup dried shrimps
3 green shallots, chopped

■ Can be made a day ahead.
■ Storage: Covered, in refrigerator.
■ Freeze: Not suitable.
■ Microwave: Suitable.

Serves 6.

1: Peel eggplants, cut into thin strips, place in top half of steamer, cook over boiling water for about 8 minutes or until just tender; drain.

2: Grind coriander, peppercorns and garlic to a paste using mortar and pestle. Combine paste with sugar, sauce, chilli, oil and juice in large bowl. Stir in eggplant; cover, stand 20 minutes.

3: Soak shrimps in cold water in bowl for 10 minutes; drain. Pound shrimps with mortar and pestle. Serve salad sprinkled with shrimps and shallots.

Plate from Royal Doulton

Main Courses

Thai food is a taste sensation! The exquisite
curry fragrances that emerge from a Thai kitchen come from the sauces,
pastes and spices that are used to enhance each special dish.
A wok is traditionally used for cooking, but a pan will do just as well
for our many quick-and-easy recipes. Here you'll find recipes for seafood,
poultry and meat that are usually served as main courses
but can also be adapted as entrees and even served at barbecues.

PEPPERED PRAWNS WITH LEEK

1 large (about 300g) leek
500g uncooked king prawns
2 tablespoons oil
1 clove garlic, crushed
1 tablespoon fish sauce
1 teaspoon brown sugar
1 teaspoon cracked black
   peppercorns
1 teaspoon chopped fresh coriander

- Recipe best made just before serving; prawns can be prepared 6 hours ahead.
- Storage: Covered, in refrigerator.
- Freeze: Not suitable.
- Microwave: Not suitable.

Serves 4.

1: Cut leek in half, cut into 3cm pieces. Add leek to pan of boiling water, boil until just tender; drain.

3: Heat oil in wok, add prawns and garlic, stir-fry for 2 minutes. Add sauce, sugar and peppercorns, stir-fry until prawns are tender. Serve prawns over leek, pour over liquid, sprinkle with coriander.

2: Shell prawns, leaving tails intact. Cut along centre back of prawns, remove vein, flatten prawns slightly.

Fabric from Gallery Nomad.
Plate from Accoutrement

STIR-FRIED SEAFOOD WITH BASIL

200g white fish fillets
8 large mussels
250g uncooked king prawns
100g squid hoods
2 cloves garlic, crushed
1 large fresh red chilli, chopped
1 tablespoon chopped
    fresh coriander root
¼ cup oil
100g scallops
2 tablespoons oyster sauce
2 tablespoons fish sauce
1 red pepper, sliced
8 green shallots, chopped
⅓ cup shredded fresh basil leaves

■ Seafood can be prepared a day ahead. Recipe best made just before serving.
■ Storage: Covered, in refrigerator.
■ Freeze: Not suitable.
■ Microwave: Not suitable.

Serves 4.

1: Chop fish into bite-sized pieces. Scrub mussels, remove beards. Shell prawns, leaving tails intact. Cut squid into 4cm squares, score inside surface of squid using a sharp knife.

2: Grind garlic, chilli and coriander to a paste using mortar and pestle. Heat oil in wok, add paste, cook, stirring, for about 1 minute, or until fragrant.

3: Add all seafood to wok, stir-fry until seafood is tender.

4: Stir in sauces, pepper, shallots and basil, stir-fry for 2 minutes.

Plate from Made in Japan

SQUID WITH RED AND GREEN PEPPERS

500g squid hoods
1 large green pepper
1 large red pepper
1 tablespoon oil
4 cloves garlic, sliced
⅓ cup water
1 tablespoon palm sugar
1 tablespoon fish sauce
1 tablespoon sweet chilli sauce

■ Can be prepared a day ahead.
■ Storage: Covered, in refrigerator.
■ Freeze: Not suitable.
■ Microwave: Not suitable.

Serves 4.

1: Cut squid hoods down side, open out flat. Score inside of hoods using a sharp knife; cut into 2cm x 3cm pieces.

3: **Just before serving,** heat oil in wok, add garlic, stir-fry 1 minute. Add squid, water, sugar and fish sauce, stir-fry for about 2 minutes or until squid curls.

2: Cut peppers into quarters, grill skin side up until skin blackens and blisters, remove skin. Cut peppers the same size as squid.

4: Stir in peppers and chilli sauce, stir-fry until heated through.

STEAMED MUSSELS WITH CREAMY FISH FILLING

24 (about 1kg) large mussels
2 tablespoons oil
1 small onion, finely chopped
2 teaspoons finely chopped
   fresh ginger
1 clove garlic, crushed
1 stem fresh lemon grass, finely
   chopped
1 teaspoon shrimp paste
500g white fish fillets, chopped
1 egg white
1 tablespoon cream
1 tablespoon chopped fresh basil
2 small fresh red chillies, sliced

■ Mussels can be prepared a day ahead.
■ Storage: Covered, in refrigerator.
■ Freeze: Not suitable.
■ Microwave: Not suitable.

Serves 6.

1: Scrub mussels; remove beards. Place mussels in pan, cover with cold water, bring to boil, simmer, covered, for about 3 minutes until mussels begin to open. Drain mussels, rinse under cold water; drain well. Remove and discard top shell from each mussel.

3: Blend or process fish, egg white and cream until smooth. Combine fish mixture, onion mixture and basil in bowl; mix well. Spoon mixture onto mussel in shells, smooth surface, top with chilli.

2: Heat oil in pan, add onion, ginger, garlic and lemon grass, cook, stirring, until onion is soft. Add paste, cook, stirring, for 1 minute; cool.

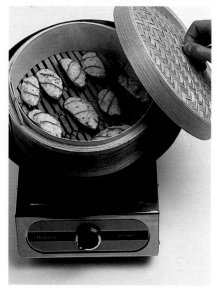

4: Just before serving, place mussels in bamboo steamer in single layer. Cook, covered tightly, over pan of boiling water, for about 3 minutes or until fish mixture is cooked through.

Dish and caneware from Java Bazaar

SEAFOOD OMELETTE

3 green shallots, chopped
2 cloves garlic, crushed
1 teaspoon ground black
    peppercorns
2 tablespoons chopped
    fresh coriander root
2 tablespoons oil
350g white fish fillets, chopped
350g cooked king prawns, shelled
¼ cup frozen peas
1 tablespoon light soy sauce
½ teaspoon fish sauce
1 tablespoon chopped fresh coriander
1 tablespoon oil, extra
6 eggs, lightly beaten
1 teaspoon cracked black
    peppercorns

■ Best made just before serving.
■ Freeze: Not suitable.
■ Microwave: Not suitable.

Serves 4.

1: Grind shallots, garlic, ground peppercorns and coriander root to a paste using mortar and pestle.

2: Heat oil in pan, add garlic paste, cook, stirring, for about 2 minutes or until fragrant. Stir in seafood, peas, sauces and fresh coriander, cook, stirring, for 2 minutes; remove from heat.

3: Heat extra oil in pan, pour in combined eggs and cracked peppercorns, cook until omelette is lightly browned underneath and top is almost set.

4: Spoon seafood mixture over half of omelette, fold omelette in half. Cook a further 2 minutes or until mixture is heated through and omelette is set.

PRAWN SALAD WITH WINE AND CHILLI DRESSING

1kg cooked king prawns, shelled
7 cos lettuce leaves

DRESSING
¼ cup fish sauce
⅓ cup lemon juice
1 tablespoon brown sugar
1 medium fresh red chilli, chopped
¼ cup dry white wine
1 stem lemon grass, finely chopped
2 tablespoons chopped
  fresh coriander

■ Salad best made 3 hours ahead.
■ Storage: Covered, in refrigerator.
■ Freeze: Not suitable.

Serves 4.

Dishes from Accoutrement

1: Combine prawns and dressing in bowl; cover, refrigerate several hours before serving. Serve salad over lettuce.

2: Dressing: Combine all ingredients in bowl; mix well.

PRAWN CURRY WITH FRESH PINEAPPLE AND ASPARAGUS

2½ cups coconut cream
½ medium (about 750g) pineapple, chopped
450g fresh asparagus, chopped
1½ teaspoons palm sugar
3 teaspoons fish sauce
375g medium cooked prawns, shelled
2 tablespoons fresh coriander leaves
2 green shallots, chopped

CURRY PASTE
1½ teaspoons dried chilli flakes
4 stems fresh lemon grass, chopped
3 teaspoons galangal powder
1 small red Spanish onion, chopped
¼ teaspoon shrimp paste
1½ teaspoons grated lime rind
¼ teaspoon paprika
pinch turmeric

- Best made just before serving. Paste can be made a week ahead.
- Storage: Covered, in refrigerator.
- Freeze: Not suitable.
- Microwave: Suitable.

Serves 4.

1: Combine curry paste and 1 cup of the coconut cream in pan, bring to boil, simmer, uncovered, for 3 minutes.

3: Add prawns and coriander, simmer until heated through. Serve curry sprinkled with shallots.

2: Stir in remaining coconut cream, pineapple, asparagus, sugar and sauce. Bring to boil, simmer, uncovered, for 2 minutes.

4: Curry Paste: Blend or process all ingredients until combined.

Bowl from Corso de Fiori

CALAMARI SALAD

500g baby calamari
⅓ cup water
1½ tablespoons fish sauce
2 tablespoons lime juice
1 small fresh red chilli, finely chopped
1 small onion, sliced
**1 tablespoon finely chopped fresh
    lemon grass**
1 tablespoon chopped fresh coriander
1 tablespoon chopped fresh mint
8 lettuce leaves

■ Can be made 6 hours ahead.
■ Storage: Covered, in refrigerator.
■ Freeze: Not suitable.
■ Microwave: Suitable.

Serves 4.

1: Gently pull heads and entrails away from bodies of calamari; discard. Remove clear quills from inside bodies; discard. Remove side flaps and skin from calamari hoods; discard.

3: Combine water, sauce, juice and chilli in pan. Bring to boil, add calamari, simmer, uncovered, for about 2 minutes or until tender, transfer mixture to bowl; cool.

2: Cut hoods into 4cm squares, score inside surface of each square using a sharp knife.

4: Add onion, lemon grass, coriander and mint to bowl, mix well, cover, refrigerate for at least 1 hour. Serve salad on lettuce.

BAKED FISH
WITH SWEET AND SOUR SAUCE

800g whole snapper
2 tablespoons fish sauce
1 tablespoon oil

SWEET AND SOUR SAUCE
1 tablespoon oil
2 cloves garlic, crushed
¼ teaspoon ground ginger
pinch chilli powder
2 tablespoons brown sugar
2 tablespoons white vinegar
2 tablespoons fish sauce
1 large tomato, chopped
1 small yellow pepper, chopped
4 baby carrots, chopped
¼ cup water

- Fish best cooked just before serving. Sauce can be made 3 hours ahead.
- Storage: Covered, in refrigerator.
- Freeze: Not suitable.
- Microwave: Sauce suitable.

Serves 4.

1: Cut 4 deep slits into each side of fish, pour fish sauce into slits.

2: Heat oil in heavy baking dish, add fish, cook on both sides to seal. Bake, covered, in moderate oven for about 30 minutes or until cooked through. Serve with hot sweet and sour sauce.

3: Sweet and Sour Sauce: Heat oil in pan, add garlic, ginger and chilli, cook, stirring, 1 minute. Add sugar, vinegar and sauce, stir over heat until sugar is dissolved. Stir in remaining ingredients, bring to boil, simmer, covered, for about 3 minutes or until vegetables are just tender.

Fabric and cane from Java Bazaar

GRILLED FISH WITH CHILLI AND CORIANDER SAUCE

3 medium fresh red chillies, chopped
1 tablespoon chopped fresh
    coriander root
3 cloves garlic, crushed
2 teaspoons sugar
4 white fish fillets
1 tablespoon oil
1 tablespoon oil, extra
1 tablespoon fish sauce
½ small chicken stock cube,
    crumbled
½ cup water
1 tablespoon lime juice
2 teaspoons cornflour
2 teaspoons water, extra

■ Best made just before serving.
■ Freeze: Not suitable.
■ Microwave: Suitable.

Serves 4.

1: Grind chillies, coriander, garlic and sugar to a paste using mortar and pestle.

2: Brush fish with oil, grill until just tender.

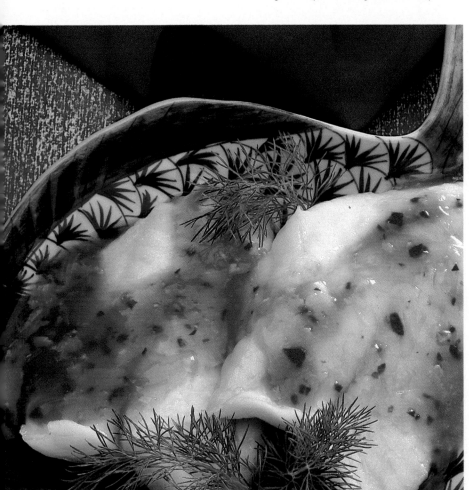

3: Heat extra oil in pan, add chilli mixture, cook, stirring, for 2 minutes. Stir in sauce, stock cube, water, juice and blended cornflour and extra water. Stir until mixture boils and thickens. Serve sauce over fish.

Plate from Accoutrement

SNAPPER CUTLETS WITH RED CURRY PASTE

¼ cup oil
4 snapper cutlets
½ cup coconut milk
1 tablespoon chopped fresh coriander

RED CURRY PASTE
2 small fresh red chillies, chopped
1 tablespoon chopped
fresh coriander root
2 cloves garlic, crushed
1 teaspoon shrimp paste
2 teaspoons chopped fresh
lemon grass
1 teaspoon ground cumin
2 teaspoons paprika
1 red Spanish onion, chopped
¼ cup lime juice

■ Recipe best made just before serving.
Paste can be made a week ahead.
■ Storage: Covered, in refrigerator.
■ Freeze: Not suitable.
■ Microwave: Not suitable.

Serves 4.

1: Heat oil in pan, add fish, cook until tender. Remove from pan.

2: Pour excess oil from pan, add paste, cook, stirring, for about 3 minutes or until fragrant. Stir in milk, bring to boil, simmer, uncovered, until slightly thickened. Serve over fish, sprinkle with coriander.

3: Red Curry Paste: Blend all ingredients until combined.

STEAMED FISH CUSTARD IN CABBAGE CUPS

1 onion, chopped
3 medium fresh red chillies, chopped
3 cloves garlic, crushed
2 tablespoons chopped fresh
    lemon grass
2 tablespoons fish sauce
500g white fish fillets, chopped
2 cups coconut cream
2 eggs, lightly beaten
½ teaspoon sugar
6 cabbage leaves, halved
1½ cups (150g) shredded
    Chinese cabbage
⅓ cup finely shredded fresh basil
3 small fresh red chillies,
    chopped, extra
2 tablespoons chopped
    fresh coriander

TOPPING
1 cup coconut cream
½ cup plain flour

■ Custards can be prepared 6 hours
    ahead.
■ Storage: Covered, in refrigerator.
■ Freeze: Not suitable.
■ Microwave: Not suitable.

Makes 8.

1: Blend or process onion, chillies, garlic, lemon grass and sauce until smooth.

2: Combine chilli mixture and fish in bowl, mix well. Stir in coconut cream, eggs and sugar; mix well.

3: Drop halved cabbage leaves into pan of boiling water, drain immediately. Line 8 greased dishes (1 cup capacity) with cabbage. Drop shredded Chinese cabbage into pan of boiling water, drain immediately. Divide shredded cabbage and basil between dishes, top with fish mixture. Spread topping over fish mixture, sprinkle with extra chillies and coriander.

4: Just before serving, place dishes in bamboo steamer, cook, covered, over boiling water for about 20 minutes or until firm. Cool, trim edges if desired, remove custards from moulds before serving.

5: Topping: Blend coconut cream and flour in bowl until smooth.

GREEN CHICKEN CURRY

750g chicken thigh fillets
200g green beans
1 cup coconut cream

GREEN CURRY PASTE
3 small fresh green chillies, chopped
3 green shallots, chopped
2 cloves garlic, crushed
¼ cup chopped fresh lemon grass
¼ cup chopped fresh coriander
2 tablespoons oil
2 tablespoons water
1 teaspoon shrimp paste
½ teaspoon ground cumin
¼ teaspoon turmeric

■ Curry best made just before serving.
  Paste can be made a week ahead.
■ Storage: Paste, covered,
  in refrigerator.
■ Freeze: Not suitable.
■ Microwave: Suitable.

Serves 4.

1: Cut chicken into thin strips. Chop beans. Add green curry paste to heated pan, cook, stirring, for about 3 minutes or until fragrant.

2: Add chicken and beans to pan, cook, stirring, for about 5 minutes or until chicken is tender. Stir in coconut cream, simmer, uncovered, for about 3 minutes or until slightly thickened.

3: Green Curry Paste: Blend or process all ingredients until smooth.

Plate and bowl from Bangkok Restaurant

CURRIED CHICKEN IN COCONUT BASKETS

1 cup water
200g chicken breast fillets
¼ cup cooked rice
1 tablespoon oil
1 onion, finely chopped
1 clove garlic, crushed
1 tablespoon curry paste
2 tablespoons chopped
**   peanuts**
1 green shallot, chopped
1 tomato, chopped
2 tablespoons chopped fresh mint
8 cos lettuce leaves, shredded

COCONUT BASKETS
⅓ cup rice flour
⅓ cup plain flour
400ml can coconut cream
oil for deep-frying

■ Can be prepared 6 hours ahead.
■ Storage: Filling, covered, in refrigerator. Coconut cups, in airtight container.
■ Freeze: Not suitable.
■ Microwave: Not suitable.

Makes 12.

1: Bring water to boil in pan, add chicken, simmer, until tender, drain. Roughly chop chicken, blend or process with rice until combined.

2: Heat oil in pan, add onion and garlic, cook, stirring, until onion is soft. Add chicken mixture, curry paste, peanuts and shallot, cook, stirring, for 3 minutes; stir in tomato and mint.

3: Just before serving, divide lettuce between coconut baskets, top with hot chicken mixture.

4: Coconut Baskets: Sift flours into bowl, gradually stir in coconut cream, beat to a smooth batter. Lightly grease outside of rounded mould (½ cup capacity). Holding edge of mould with tongs, dip mould into batter to come two-thirds up outside of mould. Deep-fry mould in hot oil until batter is just set, ease coconut basket from mould, continue frying basket until lightly browned; drain on absorbent paper. Repeat with remaining batter.

CHICKEN AND PEANUT CURRY

8 (750g) chicken thigh fillets
400ml can coconut cream

COCONUT AND PEANUT SAUCE
½ **cup peanuts**
1 clove garlic, crushed
2 teaspoons ground cumin
1 teaspoon ground coriander
1 small fresh red chilli, finely chopped
½ **teaspoon shrimp paste**
1 tablespoon light soy sauce
2 teaspoons sugar
1 tablespoon lime juice
1 tablespoon chopped fresh coriander

■ Can be made 1 hour ahead.
■ Storage: Chicken and sauce
 separately, covered, in refrigerator.
■ Freeze: Suitable.
■ Microwave: Suitable.

Serves 4.

1: Combine chicken and coconut cream in pan, bring to boil, simmer, uncovered, for about 20 minutes, or until chicken is tender. Strain chicken, reserve 1 cup liquid.

2: Slice chicken, arrange on serving plate, pour over coconut and peanut sauce.

3: Coconut and Peanut Sauce: Blend or process nuts until coarsely chopped. Combine garlic, cumin, ground coriander and chilli in pan, stir over heat for about 1 minute or until fragrant. Add reserved liquid, nuts, paste, sauce, sugar and juice, stir until combined and heated through. Serve chicken sprinkled with fresh coriander.

BAKED GARLIC QUAIL

4 quail
4 cloves garlic, crushed
3 tablespoons sambal oelek
2 tablespoons honey
2 tablespoons light soy sauce
2 teaspoons brown sugar
2 tablespoons oil

■ Quail can be prepared 2 days ahead.
■ Storage: Covered, in refrigerator.
■ Freeze: Uncooked quail suitable.
■ Microwave: Not suitable.

Serves 4.

1: Cut quail in half through centres. Combine garlic, sambal oelek, honey, sauce, sugar and oil in bowl, add quail, stir well; cover, refrigerate overnight.

2: Just before serving, place quail on rack over baking dish, bake in moderate oven for 15 minutes, increase temperature to hot, cook further 10 minutes or until quail are crisp and tender.

BAKED DUCK AND MANDARIN SALAD

No. 16 duckling
60g butter, melted
¼ teaspoon paprika
310g can mandarin segments
2 tablespoons rice vinegar
2 tablespoons oyster sauce
2 tablespoons sesame oil
2 green shallots, chopped
½ cup shredded coconut, toasted

■ Can be prepared 2 days ahead.
■ Storage: Covered, in refrigerator.
■ Freeze: Not suitable.
■ Microwave: Not suitable.

Serves 4.

1: Place duck on rack over baking dish, brush all over with combined butter and paprika. Bake duck in moderate oven for about 1½ hours or until well browned and tender, frequently brushing with butter mixture. Prick duck skin with fork when beginning to brown. Remove duck from oven; cool. Remove flesh from bones, cut flesh into thin strips.

2: Drain mandarins, reserve syrup. Combine duck, reserved syrup, vinegar, sauce and oil in bowl; cover, refrigerate several hours or overnight.

3: Just before serving, stir mandarins, shallots and toasted coconut through duck mixture.

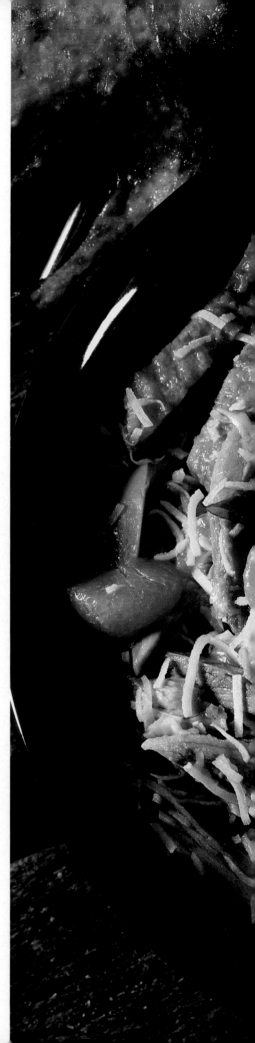

CHILLI CHICKEN WITH BASIL AND COCONUT CREAM

500g chicken breast fillets
2 tablespoons oil
1 onion, finely chopped
2 tablespoons finely chopped small
    fresh red chillies
1 cup shredded fresh basil
2 tablespoons fish sauce
1 teaspoon chopped fresh
    coriander root
1½ teaspoons sugar
1 cup coconut cream

■ Best made just before serving.
■ Freeze: Not suitable.
■ Microwave: Not suitable.

Serves 4.

1: Remove excess fat from chicken, cut chicken into 1cm strips.

2: Heat oil in wok, add onion and chillies, stir-fry until onion is soft.

3: Add chicken, stir-fry until chicken is tender. Add basil, sauce, coriander and sugar, stir-fry for 1 minute.

4: Add coconut cream, stir mixture until heated through.

CHICKEN AND BABY CORN

750g chicken thigh fillets
425g can baby corn, drained
1 tablespoon oil
4 cloves garlic, thinly sliced
2 small fresh red chillies, thinly sliced
1 tablespoon oil, extra
1 onion, chopped
1 red pepper, sliced
10 leaves Chinese broccoli, shredded
1 tablespoon fish sauce
1 tablespoon light soy sauce
1 teaspoon grated fresh ginger

■ Best made just before serving.
■ Freeze: Not suitable.
■ Microwave: Not suitable.

Serves 4.

1: Cut chicken into thin strips. Cut baby corn in half lengthways. Heat oil in wok, add garlic and chillies, stir-fry until lightly browned; remove from wok.

2: Add chicken to wok in several batches, stir-fry until tender; remove from wok.

3: Add extra oil to wok, add onion and pepper, stir-fry for 1 minute. Return chicken to pan with corn, broccoli, sauces and ginger, stir-fry until heated through. Serve topped with garlic and chillies.

Plate from Noritake

BARBECUED CHICKEN WITH SWEET VINEGAR SAUCE

1kg chicken thigh fillets
½ cup coconut milk

PASTE
4 cloves garlic, crushed
1 teaspoon cracked black peppercorns
2 teaspoons sugar
2 teaspoons turmeric
2 teaspoons paprika
1 tablespoon chopped fresh coriander root
1 teaspoon curry powder
2 small fresh red chillies, chopped
1 tablespoon oil

SWEET VINEGAR SAUCE
1 small fresh red chilli, chopped
2 cloves garlic, crushed
½ cup white vinegar
2 tablespoons raw sugar

- Recipe can be prepared 2 days ahead, paste a week ahead and sauce 6 hours ahead.
- Storage: Covered, in refrigerator.
- Freeze: Uncooked chicken suitable.
- Microwave: Not suitable.

Serves 4.

1: Cut thigh fillets in half, combine with paste in bowl; cover, refrigerate several hours or overnight.

2: Just before serving, grill chicken until tender, basting frequently with coconut milk. Serve with sweet vinegar sauce.

3: Paste: Grind all ingredients to a paste using mortar and pestle.

4: Sweet Vinegar Sauce: Grind chilli and garlic to a paste using mortar and pestle. Combine vinegar and sugar in pan, stir over heat, without boiling, until sugar is dissolved. Bring to boil, simmer, uncovered, without stirring, until syrup just begins to colour, remove from heat, cool slightly. Stir in chilli and garlic paste.

RED CHICKEN CURRY

2 tablespoons oil
4 green shallots, chopped
750g chicken thigh fillets, chopped
2 tablespoons fish sauce
1 cup coconut milk

CURRY PASTE
1 small red Spanish onion, chopped
3 cloves garlic
2 tablespoons chopped fresh
  lemon grass
3 teaspoons chopped fresh
  coriander roots
2 teaspoons dried chilli flakes
1 teaspoon galangal powder
1 teaspoon grated lime rind
½ teaspoon shrimp paste
1 dried kaffir lime leaf
3 teaspoons paprika
½ teaspoon turmeric
½ teaspoon cumin seeds
3 teaspoons oil

■ Can be made a day ahead.
■ Storage: Covered, in refrigerator.
■ Freeze: Suitable.
■ Microwave: Not suitable.

Serves 6.

1: Heat oil in wok, add ⅓ cup of the curry paste and shallots, cook, stirring, for about 2 minutes or until fragrant.

3: Stir in sauce and coconut milk, bring to boil, simmer, uncovered, until mixture is heated through.

2: Add chicken, stir-fry until just tender.

4: Curry Paste: Blend or process all ingredients until smooth.

Bowl from Royal Doulton

CHICKEN 'N' ALMOND STIR-FRY

300g chicken breast fillets
80g green beans
¼ cup oil
⅔ cup blanched almond kernels
1 teaspoon curry paste
2 tablespoons fish sauce
2 tablespoons oyster sauce
1 small fresh red chilli, finely chopped
1 tablespoon manjo mirin
1 tablespoon chopped fresh coriander
1 tablespoon chopped fresh basil

■ Best made just before serving.
■ Freeze: Not suitable.
■ Microwave: Not suitable.

Serves 6.

1: Thinly slice chicken. Cut beans into 2cm lengths.

2: Heat oil in wok, add almonds, stir-fry until lightly browned, remove almonds from wok; reserve.

3: Reheat remaining oil in wok, add chicken, stir-fry 1 minute. Add beans, paste, sauces, chilli, mirin and almonds, stir-fry until chicken is just tender; stir in coriander and basil.

China from Made in Japan

CHICKEN AND TOASTED RICE SALAD

1 cup boiling water
1 small chicken stock cube, crumbled
2 chicken breast fillets
2 tablespoons long grain rice
4 green shallots, chopped
2 large fresh red chillies,
    chopped
2 tablespoons chopped fresh mint
1 tablespoon chopped fresh coriander
1 tablespoon chopped fresh
    lemon grass
1 cos lettuce
¼ cup lime juice
1 tablespoon fish sauce
1 teaspoon sugar

■ Salad can be prepared a day ahead.
■ Storage: Covered, in refrigerator.
■ Freeze: Not suitable.
■ Microwave: Chicken suitable.

Serves 4.

1: Combine water and stock cube in pan, bring to boil, add chicken, simmer, covered, until just tender. Stand chicken in stock, for 10 minutes, drain chicken, reserve 1 tablespoon stock; discard remaining stock. Chop chicken finely; cool.

2: Place rice in dry pan, stir over heat for about 5 minutes or until lightly browned. Grind rice in batches to a fine powder using mortar and pestle.

3: Combine chicken, rice, shallots, chillies, mint, coriander and lemon grass in bowl; serve in lettuce leaves.
Just before serving, pour over combined juice, sauce, sugar and reserved stock.

CURRIED DUCK IN COCONUT MILK

1½kg duck breast fillets, halved
1 teaspoon oil
4 cups coconut milk
2 teaspoons fish sauce
2 tablespoons fresh basil leaves

CURRY PASTE
1 teaspoon dried chilli flakes
½ red Spanish onion, chopped
2 cloves garlic, crushed
**1 tablespoon chopped fresh
    lemon grass**
½ teaspoon galangal powder
**1 teaspoon fresh coriander root,
    chopped**
½ teaspoon grated lime rind
¼ teaspoon shrimp paste
1 dried kaffir lime leaf
½ teaspoon paprika
¼ teaspoon turmeric
¼ teaspoon cumin seeds
1 teaspoon oil, approximately

■ Recipe can be prepared a day ahead.
  Paste can be made a week ahead.
■ Storage: Covered, in refrigerator.
■ Freeze: Not suitable.
■ Microwave: Not suitable.

Serves 6.

1: Prick duck skin with fork. Heat oil in pan, place duck skin side down in pan, cook slowly until the fat has cooked out of the skin and the skin is well browned. This will take about 15 minutes. Remove duck from pan, drain.

2: Place 2 cups of coconut milk in pan, bring to the boil, simmer 10 minutes. Add duck, simmer further 10 minutes.

3: Combine curry paste, sauce and remaining coconut milk in bowl, add to duck mixture, simmer until duck is tender. **Just before serving,** stir in basil leaves.

4: Curry Paste: Blend or process all ingredients with enough oil to form a thick paste consistency.

QUAIL WITH FRESH CHILLI AND BASIL

4 quail
oil for deep-frying
1 clove garlic, crushed
1 small fresh red chilli, finely chopped
1 tablespoon oyster sauce
1 tablespoon fish sauce
2 tablespoons shredded fresh basil

■ Best made just before serving.
■ Freeze: Not suitable.
■ Microwave: Not suitable.

Serves 4.

1: Cut quail in half, cut away backbone. Cut each quail half into 3 portions.

2: Deep-fry quail pieces in hot oil in wok until well browned and tender; drain on absorbent paper.

3: Drain oil from wok, leave 1 tablespoon oil in wok. Add garlic, chilli and sauces to wok, cook, stirring, for 1 minute. Return quail to wok, stir until heated through. **Just before serving**, stir in basil.

Plates from Limoges

CHICKEN IN COCONUT MILK

No. 16 chicken
1 litre (4 cups) coconut milk
1 teaspoon dried chilli flakes
2 tablespoons chopped peanuts
¼ teaspoon black peppercorns
2 stems fresh lemon grass, chopped
4 green shallots, chopped
2 cloves garlic, crushed
1 tablespoon brown sugar
1 teaspoon shrimp paste
2 teaspoons oil
1 cup coconut milk, extra

■ Can be prepared a day ahead.
■ Storage: Covered, in refrigerator.
■ Freeze: Not suitable.
■ Microwave: Suitable.

Serves 4.

1: Combine chicken and coconut milk in pan, bring to boil, simmer, covered, for 45 minutes. Drain chicken; discard coconut milk. Remove chicken flesh from bones; discard bones and skin.

2: Blend chilli, peanuts, peppercorns, lemon grass, shallots, garlic, sugar and paste until mixture is well combined.

3: Just before serving, heat oil in pan, stir in peanut mixture, cook, stirring, for about 2 minutes or until fragrant. Stir in extra coconut milk and chicken, stir until heated through.

DEEP-FRIED WINGS WITH MINCE STUFFING

12 large (about 1.3kg) chicken wings
500g minced chicken
2 green shallots, chopped
2 teaspoons chopped fresh ginger
2 cloves garlic, crushed
1 small fresh red chilli, chopped
1 tablespoon cornflour
cornflour, extra
1 egg, lightly beaten
1 cup packaged breadcrumbs
oil for deep-frying

SWEET CHILLI PEANUT SAUCE
½ cup sugar
2 tablespoons water
2 tablespoons white vinegar
1 tablespoon chopped peanuts
1 small fresh red chilli, chopped

- Can be prepared 2 days ahead.
- Storage: Covered, in refrigerator.
- Freeze: Uncooked crumbed wings suitable.
- Microwave: Not suitable.

Makes 12.

1: Holding end of large third joint of wings, trim around bone with knife. Cut, scrape and push meat down to middle joint, without cutting skin. Twist bone and remove; discard bone.

3: Toss wings in extra cornflour, shake away excess cornflour. Dip into egg, then breadcrumbs.

Just before serving, deep-fry wings in hot oil until well browned and tender; drain on absorbent paper. Serve with sweet chilli peanut sauce.

2: Blend or process mince, shallots, ginger, garlic, chilli and cornflour until combined. Using fingers, fill cavities of wings with mixture, secure ends with toothpicks.

4: Sweet Chilli Peanut Sauce: Combine sugar and water in pan, stir over heat until sugar is dissolved. Bring to boil, simmer, uncovered, for 2 minutes; cool. Stir in vinegar, peanuts and chilli.

BEEF CURRY WITH BAMBOO SHOOTS

2 tablespoons oil
1.2kg rump steak, thinly sliced
397g can bamboo shoots,
    drained, sliced
2 small fresh red chillies, chopped
2 small fresh green chillies, chopped
2 tablespoons fish sauce
1 dried kaffir lime leaf
1 teaspoon brown sugar
2 tablespoons chopped fresh basil

CURRY PASTE
5 dried red chillies
1 tablespoon chopped dried galangal
1 tablespoon chopped dried kaffir
    lime peel
1 cup water
2 green shallots, chopped
2 cloves garlic, crushed
2 teaspoons grated lemon rind
1 tablespoon finely chopped fresh
    lemon grass
1 teaspoon finely chopped
    fresh ginger

■ Curry best made close to serving.
  Paste can be made 2 weeks ahead.
■ Storage: Covered, in refrigerator.
■ Freeze: Curry suitable; paste not
  suitable.
■ Microwave: Not suitable.

Serves 8.

1: Heat oil in large wok, add steak, stir-fry until browned all over. Add ¼ cup curry paste, stir for 2 minutes.

2: Add bamboo shoots, chillies, sauce, lime leaf and sugar, stir-fry until steak is tender; stir in basil.

3: Curry Paste: Combine chillies, galangal and peel in bowl, cover with water; cover, stand several hours. Drain peel mixture, reserve ½ cup liquid. Blend or process peel mixture, reserved liquid, shallots, garlic, rind, lemon grass and ginger until smooth.

Bowl from Made in Japan. Fabric and spoon from Gallery Nomad

BEEF WITH OYSTER SAUCE

1 bunch bok choy
½ bunch Chinese broccoli
500g rump steak
2 tablespoons oil
2 cloves garlic, crushed
150g snow peas
425g can baby corn, drained
6 green shallots, chopped
2 tablespoons oyster sauce
1 tablespoon fish sauce
1 tablespoon sugar

■ Recipe best made just before serving.
■ Freeze: Not suitable.
■ Microwave: Bok choy and broccoli suitable.

Serves 4.

1: Break bok choy and broccoli into large pieces, steam or microwave until just tender; drain well.

2: Cut steak into thin strips. Heat oil in wok, add garlic and steak; stir-fry until steak is just browned.

3: Add peas, corn, shallots, sauces and sugar, stir-fry until peas are just tender. Serve over bok choy and broccoli.

BEEF CURRY WITH RED AND GREEN CHILLIES

1kg rump steak
1 small fresh red chilli
1 small fresh green chilli
2 cups coconut milk
¼ cup coconut cream
2 teaspoons fish sauce
2 tablespoons raw sugar
4 green shallots, chopped
2 tablespoons oil

CURRY PASTE
2 small fresh red chillies, chopped
3 cloves garlic, crushed
1 teaspoon chopped fresh lemon grass
1 teaspoon grated lime rind
1 teaspoon dried galangal
¼ teaspoon ground cardamom
2 green shallots, chopped
½ teaspoon cracked black peppercorns
2 teaspoons chopped fresh coriander root
½ teaspoon shrimp paste
2 teaspoons lime juice

■ Curry best made just before serving. Paste can be made a week ahead.
■ Storage: Covered, in refrigerator.
■ Freeze: Not suitable.
■ Microwave: Not suitable.

Serves 6.

1: Cut steak into 5cm slices. Cut chillies into thin strips. Heat coconut milk in pan, add steak, bring to boil, simmer, uncovered, for about 15 minutes or until steak is tender.

2: Heat coconut cream in separate pan, add curry paste, simmer, uncovered, for about 1 minute or until fragrant.

3: Stir paste mixture into steak mixture, bring to boil, simmer, uncovered, until liquid is almost evaporated. Stir in sauce, sugar and shallots.

4: Heat oil in pan, add chillies, cook, stirring, for about 2 minutes or until chillies are crisp. Sprinkle cooked chillies over curry just before serving.

5: Curry Paste: Grind all ingredients to a paste using mortar and pestle.

BEEF AND MUSHROOM SALAD

60g (1½ cups) dried mushrooms
600g piece rump steak
2 tablespoons oil
1 red pepper, sliced
½ cup roasted cashews
9 large English spinach leaves,
    shredded

DRESSING
2 tablespoons sesame oil
2 tablespoons fish sauce
2 tablespoons sweet sherry
2 tablespoons oyster sauce

■ Steak can be prepared a day ahead.
■ Storage: Covered, in refrigerator.
■ Freeze: Not suitable.
■ Microwave: Not suitable.

Serves 4.

1: Place mushrooms in bowl, cover with warm water, stand 20 minutes. Drain mushrooms, discard stems, cut caps into thin slices. Trim excess fat from steak. Heat oil in pan, add steak, cook until browned on both sides and medium rare; cool. Cut steak into thin strips.

2: Just before serving, combine steak, mushrooms, pepper, nuts and spinach in bowl, add dressing; toss well.

3: Dressing: Combine all ingredients in bowl; mix well.

Left: Statuette and cloth from Private Life

STIR-FRIED STEAK WITH GREEN BEANS

180g green beans
1 tablespoon oil
1 onion, chopped
2 cloves garlic, crushed
1 large fresh green chilli, chopped
1 large fresh red chilli, chopped
1 tablespoon oil, extra
500g rump steak, thinly sliced
1 tablespoon fish sauce
1 tablespoon chopped fresh coriander
1 teaspoon sugar

■ Best made close to serving.
■ Freeze: Not suitable.
■ Microwave: Not suitable.

Serves 4.

1: Slice beans diagonally. Heat oil in wok, add onion, garlic, chillies and beans, stir-fry until beans are just tender; remove from wok.

2: Add extra oil to wok, add steak, stir-fry until tender.

3: Return bean mixture to wok with sauce, coriander and sugar, stir-fry for about 2 minutes, or until heated through.

DRY BEEF CURRY WITH ONIONS AND PEANUTS

1kg chuck steak, chopped
3 cups coconut milk
1 cup finely ground peanuts
1 tablespoon fish sauce
2 teaspoons tamarind sauce
6 (150g) baby onions
¼ teaspoon ground cloves
¼ teaspoon ground cardamom
¼ teaspoon ground cinnamon
1½ tablespoons lime juice
1 teaspoon palm sugar

CURRY PASTE
2 teaspoons dried chilli flakes
1 red Spanish onion, chopped
3 cloves garlic, crushed
2 tablespoons chopped fresh
    lemon grass
1 teaspoon galangal powder
2 teaspoons chopped fresh
    coriander root
1 teaspoon grated lime rind
½ teaspoon shrimp paste
1 dried kaffir lime leaf
1 teaspoon paprika
½ teaspoon turmeric
½ teaspoon cumin seeds
2 teaspoons oil, approximately

■ Recipe can be prepared a day ahead.
    Paste can be made a week ahead.
■ Storage: Covered, in refrigerator.
■ Freeze: Suitable.
■ Microwave: Not suitable.

Serves 6.

1: Combine beef, coconut milk and nuts in pan, bring to the boil, simmer, covered, 1 hour, stirring occasionally.

2: Stir in curry paste, sauces, onions, spices, juice and sugar, simmer, uncovered, 10 minutes.

3: Curry Paste: Blend or process all ingredients with enough oil to form a paste consistency.

Bowl from Gallery Nomad

PORK CURRY WITH EGGPLANT

750g pork fillet
¼ cup coconut cream
2½ cups coconut milk
1 medium eggplant, chopped
1 tablespoon fish sauce
1½ teaspoons grated fresh ginger
2 teaspoons palm sugar
3 small fresh green chillies, sliced
3 small fresh red chillies, sliced
¼ cup fresh basil leaves

CURRY PASTE
2 teaspoons dried chilli flakes
1 red Spanish onion, chopped
3 cloves garlic, crushed
2 tablespoons chopped fresh
**   lemon grass**
1 teaspoon galangal powder
2 teaspoons chopped fresh
**   coriander root**
1 teaspoon grated lime rind
½ teaspoon shrimp paste
1 dried kaffir lime leaf
1 teaspoon paprika
½ teaspoon turmeric
½ teaspoon cumin seeds
2 teaspoons oil, approximately

■ Can be prepared a day ahead. Paste
  can be made a week ahead.
■ Storage: Covered, in refrigerator.
■ Freeze: Not suitable.
■ Microwave: Suitable.

Serves 6.

1: Cut pork into 2cm slices, then cut slices
in half. Combine coconut cream and curry
paste in pan, cook for 1 minute or until
fragrant. Add pork, cook 5 minutes.

2: Stir in coconut milk, eggplant, sauce,
ginger, sugar and chillies. Bring to the boil,
simmer, covered, until pork is tender.
Just before serving, stir in basil.

3: Curry Paste: Blend or process all
ingredients with enough oil to form a
paste consistency.

MINCED PORK SALAD WITH GINGER AND MINT

500g pork fillets, chopped
1 tablespoon oil
1 tablespoon water
¼ cup lime juice
2 tablespoons fish sauce
2 small fresh red chillies, chopped
1 small onion, finely sliced
4 green shallots, chopped
¼ cup peanuts
1 tablespoon grated fresh ginger
2 tablespoons chopped fresh mint
2 tablespoons fresh coriander leaves
8 cos lettuce leaves
1 tablespoon chopped peanuts, extra
sliced fresh ginger, extra
fresh coriander leaves, extra

■ Pork salad can be made a day ahead.
■ Storage: Covered, in refrigerator.
■ Freeze: Not suitable.
■ Microwave: Not suitable.

Serves 4.

1: Process pork until finely minced. Heat oil in pan, add pork and water, cook, stirring, until pork is tender.

2: Remove pork from heat, stir in juice, sauce and chillies; cool.

3: Combine pork mixture with onion, shallots, nuts, ginger, mint and coriander in bowl. Serve pork salad over lettuce, sprinkled with extra chopped nuts, extra ginger and extra coriander.

SWEET AND SOUR PORK SPARE RIBS

1 tablespoon oil
2 cloves garlic, crushed
½ red Spanish onion, chopped
2 tablespoons sugar
2 tablespoons lime juice
¼ cup pineapple juice
2 teaspoons fish sauce
1 tablespoon oyster sauce
⅓ cup tomato sauce
1 tablespoon sweet chilli sauce
1 tablespoon white vinegar
1kg pork spare ribs

■ Sauce can be made 2 days ahead.
■ Storage: Sauce, covered, in refrigerator.
■ Freeze: Cooked and uncooked ribs, suitable.
■ Microwave: Not suitable.

Serves 4.

1: Heat oil in pan, add garlic and onion, cook, stirring, until onion is soft. Stir in combined sugar, juices, sauces and vinegar; bring to boil, simmer, uncovered, 2 minutes or until slightly thickened.

2: Place spare ribs on rack over baking dish, brush with sweet and sour sauce. Bake in hot oven for 10 minutes, reduce heat to moderately hot, bake about 15 minutes or until pork is crisp and cooked through. Turn and baste ribs several times during cooking.

STEAMED MINCED PORK CUPS

250g minced pork
180g minced chicken
170g can crab meat, drained
¼ cup coconut milk
4 green shallots, chopped
1 tablespoon chopped fresh coriander
1 stem fresh lemon grass, chopped
3 cloves garlic, crushed
2 tablespoons fish sauce
½ teaspoon palm sugar
¼ teaspoon cracked black
　　peppercorns
2 eggs, separated
4 small green cucumbers, chopped
2 cups (200g) bean sprouts
2 small red peppers, chopped

■ Can be prepared a day ahead.
■ Storage: Covered, in refrigerator.
■ Freeze: Uncooked cups suitable.
■ Microwave: Not suitable.

Serves 6.

1: Blend or process pork, chicken, crab, coconut milk, shallots, coriander, lemon grass, garlic, sauce, sugar and peppercorns until combined; transfer mixture to bowl.

2: Beat egg whites with 1 of the egg yolks in small bowl with electric mixer until thick and creamy, fold into pork mixture.

3: Spoon pork mixture into 6 (½ cup capacity) ungreased bowls, press in firmly, smooth tops. Brush tops with remaining egg yolk.

4: Just before serving, place bowls in bamboo steamer, cook, covered, over boiling water for about 20 minutes or until cooked through; cool. Turn out cups, cut into wedges. Serve over combined cucumber, sprouts and peppers.

LAMB WITH BASIL AND VEGETABLES

2 cloves garlic
2 large fresh red chillies
1 carrot
1 onion
1 tablespoon oil
1 tablespoon oil, extra
1½ tablespoons tandoori curry paste
500g lamb fillet, thinly sliced
230g can bamboo shoots,
    drained, sliced
4 green shallots, chopped
⅓ cup shredded fresh basil
1 tablespoon fish sauce

■ Best made close to serving.
■ Freeze: Not suitable.
■ Microwave: Not suitable.

Serves 4.

1: Cut garlic, chillies and carrot into thin strips. Cut onion into wedges.

2: Heat oil in wok, add garlic and chillies, stir-fry until lightly browned; remove from wok. Reheat wok, add onion, stir-fry until soft, remove from wok.

3: Add extra oil to wok, heat oil, add curry paste, cook 1 minute. Add lamb in batches, stir-fry until lamb is tender.

4: Return lamb and onion to wok with remaining ingredients, stir-fry until heated through. Serve lamb mixture topped with garlic and chilli.

Accessories from Java Bazaar

LAMB FILLET IN CHILLI AND COCONUT MILK

800g lamb fillets
1 tablespoon oil
3 small fresh red chillies, chopped
1½ cups coconut milk
2 tablespoons fish sauce
1 teaspoon palm sugar
2 tablespoons lime juice
½ cup peanuts, finely chopped
2 tablespoons chopped
**   fresh coriander**

CURRY PASTE
3 dried chillies, chopped
1 dried kaffir lime leaf
½ teaspoon galangal powder
1 stem fresh lemon grass, chopped
1 teaspoon shrimp powder
⅓ cup boiling water
4 green shallots, chopped
2 cloves garlic, crushed
¼ teaspoon ground coriander
1 tablespoon fish sauce
2 tablespoons crunchy peanut butter

■ Recipe can be made several hours ahead. Paste can be made 2 weeks ahead.
■ Storage: Covered, in refrigerator. Paste, covered, in refrigerator.
■ Freeze: Cooked recipe suitable.
■ Microwave: Not suitable.

Serves 4.

1: Cut each lamb fillet into 3 portions, pound each piece with mallet until ½cm thick. Heat oil in pan, add lamb, cook until well browned all over; remove from pan.

3: Add coconut milk, sauce, sugar, juice and nuts, stir until boiling. Add lamb to pan, simmer, covered, for about 5 minutes or until lamb is tender.
Just before serving, stir in coriander.

2: Combine 2 tablespoons of curry paste with chillies in pan, stir over heat for about 2 minutes or until fragrant.

4: Curry Paste: Combine chillies, lime leaf, galangal, lemon grass, shrimp powder and water in bowl; stand 20 minutes. Drain chilli mixture, discard liquid. Blend or process chilli mixture with remaining ingredients until a coarse paste forms.

Rice & Noodles

Rice is the staple of the Thai people's diet. Freshly cooked plain steamed rice is served with curries and soups as part of a meal, while more elaborate preparations - fried rice as well as fried noodles - are served as light meals in their own right. Rice is always cooked using the absorption method and the recipe we have included will ensure fluffy, fragrant rice every time.

FRIED RICE STICKS WITH COCONUT SAUCE

200g rice sticks
1 carrot
1 tablespoon oil
2 cloves garlic, crushed
1 onion, chopped
250g pork fillet, thinly sliced
2 cups coconut milk
½ cup coconut cream
2 teaspoons palm sugar
2 teaspoons fish sauce
2 teaspoons tamarind sauce
1 tablespoon chopped fresh chives
100g firm tofu, chopped
fresh coriander leaves

■ Best made close to serving time.
■ Freeze: Not suitable.
■ Microwave: Not suitable.

Serves 4.

1: Place rice sticks in bowl; cover with hot water, stand 15 minutes.

3: Stir in coconut milk, coconut cream, sugar, sauces and carrot, simmer 5 minutes. Remove ⅓ cup liquid from wok.

2: Chop carrot into thin strips. Heat oil in wok, add garlic, onion and pork, cook until pork is browned and tender.

4: Stir in drained rice sticks; cook 5 minutes or until tender. Stir in chives. Place rice sticks on serving dish, spoon over reserved liquid, serve topped with tofu and coriander.

Dish from Morgan Imports

NOODLES WITH PRAWNS AND GREEN PEPPER

1 tablespoon oil
2 cloves garlic, crushed
1 large fresh red chilli, sliced
1 green pepper, sliced
2 green shallots, chopped
2 tablespoons oyster sauce
1 tablespoon fish sauce
2 teaspoons sugar
1 small chicken stock cube, crumbled
2 teaspoons cornflour
1 cup water
250g small cooked prawns, shelled
500g fresh rice noodles

■ Best made close to serving.
■ Freeze: Not suitable.
■ Microwave: Suitable.

Serves 6.

1: Heat oil in wok, add garlic, chilli, pepper and shallots, stir-fry for 1 minute; remove from wok.

2: Combine sauces, sugar and stock cube in wok. Blend cornflour with water, add mixture to wok. Stir over heat until mixture boils and thickens.

3: Return vegetables to wok with prawns and noodles, stir-fry until heated through.

Left: Tray from Java Bazaar. Dish and accessories from Morgan Imports

FRIED NOODLES WITH GARLIC PORK

175g dried egg noodles
2 tablespoons oil
2 cloves garlic, crushed
250g pork fillet, chopped
½ cup chopped peanuts
¼ cup dried shrimps
6 green shallots, chopped
2 tablespoons fish sauce
1 teaspoon palm sugar
1 small fresh red chilli, finely chopped
2 tablespoons lime juice
2 tablespoons chopped fresh
    coriander

■ Best made just before serving.
■ Freeze: Not suitable.
■ Microwave: Noodles suitable.

Serves 4.

1: Add noodles to large pan of boiling water, boil, uncovered, for about 5 minutes or until tender; drain well.

2: Heat oil in wok, add garlic and pork, stir-fry over heat until pork is browned.

3: Add nuts, shrimps, shallots, sauce, sugar, chilli and juice, stir-fry 1 minute.

4: Stir in noodles and coriander, stir-fry until heated through.

SPICY FRIED RICE

1 cup (200g) long grain rice
10g (¼ cup) dried mushrooms
400g can baby corn, drained
500g cooked king prawns, shelled
¼ cup oil
3 eggs, lightly beaten
1 onion, chopped
2 cloves garlic, crushed
1 pork butterfly steak, chopped
2 seafood sticks, sliced
1 green pepper, chopped
1 tablespoon curry paste
2 tablespoons light soy sauce
1 tablespoon fish sauce
1 tablespoon chopped fresh coriander

■ Rice can be prepared a day ahead.
■ Storage: Covered, in refrigerator.
■ Freeze: Not suitable.
■ Microwave: Not suitable.

Serves 6.

1: Rinse rice under cold water, drain. Add rice to large pan of boiling water. Boil, uncovered, for about 10 minutes or until tender, drain, rinse rice under cold water; drain well.

2: Place mushrooms in bowl, cover with warm water, stand 20 minutes. Drain mushrooms, discard stems, cut caps into thin slices. Cut corn into quarters. Cut prawns in half lengthways.

3: Just before serving, heat 1 table-spoon of the oil in wok, add eggs, stir uncooked egg to outside edge of wok, cook until firm. Remove omelette from wok, roll up firmly, cut into thin slices.

4: Heat remaining oil in wok, add onion and garlic, stir-fry 30 seconds. Add pork, stir-fry until browned. Add prawns, seafood sticks, pepper and paste, stir-fry 2 minutes. Add rice, sauces and coriander, stir-fry until heated through. Serve rice topped with omelette slices.

Fabric from Gallery Nomad

STEAMED JASMINE RICE

2 cups jasmine rice
4½ cups water

- Can be made a day ahead.
- Storage: Covered, in refrigerator.
- Freeze: Suitable.
- Microwave: Suitable.

Serves 4.

1: Rinse rice in strainer under cold water until water is clear. Combine water and rice in heavy-based pan, bring to boil, stirring, reduce heat, simmer gently, covered with a tight fitting lid, 12 minutes. Remove from heat, stand, covered, 10 minutes. It is important not to remove lid during cooking and steaming.

2: Fluff rice with fork or chopsticks.

FRIED RICE WITH CHICKEN

2 cups long grain rice
¼ cup oil
1 medium onion, chopped
2 cloves garlic, crushed
1 small red pepper, chopped
1 cup chopped cooked chicken
2 eggs, lightly beaten
¼ cup fish sauce
1 tablespoon chopped fresh coriander
3 green shallots, chopped

■ Best made close to serving;
   rice best prepared a day ahead.
■ Storage: Covered, in refrigerator.
■ Freeze: Not suitable.
■ Microwave: Not suitable.

Serves 4.

1: Add rice to large pan of boiling water, boil, uncovered, for about 12 minutes or until just tender, drain. Rinse rice under cold water; drain well. Spread rice over tray, cover, refrigerate overnight. Heat oil in wok, add onion, cook, stirring, until soft. Stir in garlic and pepper, stir-fry until pepper is soft. Add rice and chicken, stir-fry until heated through.

2: Stir in eggs quickly, stir-fry until cooked; stir in sauce. Serve, sprinkled with coriander and shallots.

SEAFOOD, PORK AND CHICKEN NOODLES

1 teaspoon chopped fresh
    coriander root
½ teaspoon cracked black
    peppercorns
4 cloves garlic, crushed
3 medium fresh red chillies,
    chopped
2 tablespoons light soy sauce
2 tablespoons white vinegar
2 tablespoons lime juice
1½ tablespoons sugar
300g uncooked prawns
100g squid hoods
150g pork fillet
200g chicken breast fillet
150g rice vermicelli
1 small red pepper, sliced
3 green shallots, chopped
¼ cup fresh coriander leaves
3 hard-boiled eggs, quartered

■ Noodles can be cooked a day ahead.
■ Storage: Covered, in refrigerator.
■ Freeze: Not suitable.
■ Microwave: Not suitable.

Serves 6.

1: Grind coriander root, peppercorns, garlic and chillies into a paste using mortar and pestle. Place paste in jar with sauce, vinegar, juice and sugar, shake well.

2: Shell prawns, leaving tails intact. Cut squid into 2cm square pieces, score inside surface with a sharp knife. Poach prawns, squid, pork and chicken separately in a pan of simmering water until tender; drain, cut chicken and pork into pieces.

3: Cook vermicelli in a pan of boiling water for about 3 minutes or until tender; drain.

4: Cut vermicelli into shorter lengths with scissors. Combine vermicelli in bowl with pork, chicken, seafood, pepper, shallots and coriander leaves. Stir in vinegar mixture. Serve warm or cold topped with egg.

NOODLES WITH GARLIC, BEEF AND BROCCOLI

250g rice vermicelli
450g rump steak
2 tablespoons oil
2 tablespoons dark soy sauce
5 cloves garlic, sliced
700g broccoli, chopped
1 tablespoon oyster sauce
1 tablespoon cornflour
¾ cup water
¼ cup white vinegar
1 tablespoon sugar
1 small red chilli, chopped
1 small green chilli, chopped

- Best made close to serving.
- Storage: Covered, in refrigerator.
- Freeze: Not suitable.
- Microwave: Not suitable.

Serves 4.

1: Soak vermicelli in warm water for 15 minutes, drain well. Slice steak into 1cm x 5cm strips.

2: Heat 1 tablespoon of the oil in wok, add vermicelli and soy sauce, stir-fry for 2 minutes, remove from wok.

3: Heat remaining oil in wok, add garlic and steak, stir-fry until steak is browned all over.

4: Stir in broccoli, oyster sauce, blended cornflour and water, vinegar and sugar, stir-fry until mixture boils and thickens. Serve broccoli over noodles sprinkled with chillies.

SWEET PUFFED NOODLES

100g rice vermicelli
oil for deep-frying
3 teaspoons oil, extra
2 cloves garlic, crushed
100g minced chicken
1 egg, lightly beaten
¼ cup sugar
2 tablespoons water
1 tablespoon white vinegar
300g small cooked prawns, shelled
2 green shallots, chopped

■ Best made just before serving.
■ Freeze: Not suitable.
■ Microwave: Not suitable.

Serves 6.

Bowl from Made in Japan

1: Deep-fry vermicelli in hot oil in batches until puffed; drain on absorbent paper.

2: Heat 2 teaspoons of the extra oil in small pan, add garlic, cook, stirring, 1 minute. Add chicken, cook, stirring, further minute or until cooked; remove from pan.

3: Heat remaining extra oil in pan, add egg, swirl to coat base of pan. Cook 1 minute, turn omelette, cook on other side, remove, roll omelette firmly, cut into 5mm slices.

4: Combine sugar, water and vinegar in small pan, stir over heat until sugar is dissolved. Combine noodles, chicken mixture, prawns, shallots, omelette strips and sugar syrup in large bowl, toss lightly.

Desserts

Desserts are not usually served after a Thai meal
but often appear at banquets and festive occasions;
a wide variety of delightful sweets are also sold by street vendors.
You'll find that our recipes are delicious at any time – either
as after-dinner desserts or in-between snacks.

STICKY RICE CUSTARD

½ cup short grain rice
2 tablespoons brown sugar
1 cup coconut milk
1 cup water
1 teaspoon sesame seeds, toasted

CUSTARD
4 eggs
1 cup coconut milk
2 tablespoons sugar

- Custards can be made 2 days ahead.
- Storage: Covered, in refrigerator.
- Freeze: Not suitable.
- Microwave: Not suitable.

Makes 6.

1: Lightly grease 6 (½ cup capacity) ovenproof dishes. Combine rice, sugar, coconut milk and water in pan, stir over heat until sugar is dissolved. Bring to boil, simmer, uncovered, stirring occasionally, for about 20 minutes, or until nearly all the liquid has been absorbed.

3: Place dishes in baking dish, pour in enough hot water to come halfway up sides of dishes; cover dishes with foil. Bake in moderate oven for about 1 hour until custard is set. Remove dishes from water, cool, refrigerate until cold. Serve custards with fresh fruit, if desired.

2: Spread rice evenly into prepared dishes. Pour custard evenly over rice. Sprinkle with seeds.

4: Custard: Whisk eggs, milk and sugar together in bowl.

COCONUT ROSE CUSTARD

1²⁄₃ cups coconut cream
5 eggs, lightly beaten
½ cup brown sugar, firmly packed
1 tablespoon rose water
2 tablespoons coconut

- Can be made a day ahead.
- Storage: Covered, in refrigerator.
- Freeze: Not suitable.
- Microwave: Not suitable.

Serves 6.

1: Combine all ingredients in pan, stir over heat until warm, do not boil.

2: Pour mixture into greased 22cm shallow round ovenproof dish. Place dish in baking dish, pour in enough boiling water to come halfway up side of dish.

3: Bake in moderate oven for about 20 minutes or until centre of custard is just set. Remove custard from baking dish, cool. Refrigerate custard before serving.
Just before serving, Cut into wedges and sprinkle with extra coconut, if desired.

COCONUT BANANAS WITH CARAMEL SAUCE

4 firm bananas
plain flour
2 eggs, lightly beaten
1 cup (70g) shredded coconut
2 tablespoons packaged
    breadcrumbs
oil for deep-frying

CARAMEL SAUCE
½ cup brown sugar, firmly packed
½ cup castor sugar
½ cup water
340g can coconut milk
1 tablespoon arrowroot
1 tablespoon water, extra
20g butter

■ Sauce can be made 3 hours ahead.
■ Storage: Sauce, covered,
   in refrigerator.
■ Freeze: Not suitable.
■ Microwave: Not suitable.

Serves 4.

1: Cut bananas in half lengthways, toss in flour, shake away excess flour. Dip bananas in eggs, then in combined coconut and breadcrumbs.
Just before serving, deep-fry bananas in hot oil until lightly browned; drain on absorbent paper. Serve hot bananas with caramel sauce.

2: Caramel Sauce: Combine sugars and water in pan, stir over heat, without boiling, until sugars are dissolved. Bring to boil, boil, uncovered, for about 8 minutes, or until golden brown. Stir in coconut milk and blended arrowroot and extra water, stir until sauce thickens slightly, remove from heat, add butter, stir until melted.

TROPICAL FRUITS IN LIME SYRUP

2 cups sugar
2 cups water
¼ cup lime juice
½ rockmelon, sliced
½ honeydew melon, sliced
1 small papaw, sliced
1 small pineapple, sliced
375g lychees, pitted

■ Syrup can be prepared 2 days ahead.
■ Storage: Covered, in refrigerator.
■ Freeze: Not suitable.
■ Microwave: Not suitable.

Serves 4.

1: Combine sugar, water and lime juice in pan, stir over heat without boiling until sugar is dissolved. Bring to the boil, boil rapidly, uncovered, without stirring for about 20 minutes or until syrup is thick; cool, refrigerate.

2: **Just before serving,** pour syrup over fruit; mix gently.

COCONUT CUSTARD IN PUMPKIN SHELLS

2½ cups hot water
2 cups coconut
3 golden nugget pumpkins
5 eggs
½ cup brown sugar, firmly packed
1 teaspoon rosewater

- Can be made a day ahead.
- Storage: Covered, in refrigerator.
- Freeze: Not suitable.
- Microwave: Not suitable.

Serves 4.

1: Pour water over coconut in bowl; cover, stand for 1 hour. Blend or process mixture for about 30 seconds, strain through fine strainer or muslin to give 1 cup coconut milk.

2: Cut small rounds from tops of pumpkins, reserve. Remove seeds and membranes with spoon, leaving flesh intact. Trim bases so pumpkins can sit flat.

3: Place pumpkin in baking dish. Whisk eggs lghtly with coconut milk, sugar and rosewater. Pour into pumpkin shells, replace tops.

4: Pour enough hot water into baking dish to come halfway up sides of pumpkin shells, bake in moderately slow oven for about 1¼ hours or until custard is set. Remove pumpkins from baking dish, cool; refrigerate until cold.

5: Discard pumpkin tops, cut pumpkins into quarters to serve.

MANGO ICE-CREAM

You will need 4 ripe mangoes
for this recipe.
1 tablespoon gelatine
¼ cup water
3 cups (600g) chopped mango
¾ cup castor sugar
1 tablespoon orange juice
300ml carton thickened cream

- ■ Can be made a week ahead.
- ■ Storage: Covered, in freezer.
- ■ Freeze: Suitable.
- ■ Microwave: Gelatine suitable.

Serves 4.

1: Soften gelatine in water in cup, stir over simmering water until dissolved. Pour gelatine mixture into bowl, stir in mango, sugar and orange juice, stir until sugar is dissolved. Place mixture in lamington pan; cover, freeze for about 1 hour or until firm, process until pale in colour.

2: Whip cream until soft peaks form, fold into mango mixture. Return to lamington pan; cover, freeze several hours or overnight. Remove from freezer 15 minutes before serving.

SWEET POTATO AND CARDAMOM ICE-CREAM

350g kumara, finely chopped
2 cups milk
¼ cup sugar
1½ teaspoons ground cardamom
400g can sweetened condensed milk
300ml carton thickened cream

■ Can be made a week ahead.
■ Storage: Covered, in freezer.
■ Microwave: Suitable.

Serves 6.

1: Combine kumara, milk, sugar and cardamom in pan; stir without boiling until sugar is dissolved. Bring to boil, simmer, covered, for about 15 minutes or until kumara is tender; cool.

2: Blend or process kumara mixture in batches until smooth, blend in condensed milk. Pour into lamington pan; cover, freeze several hours or until partially set.

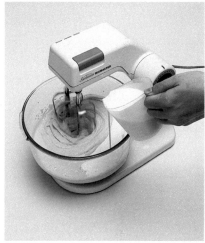

3: Beat kumara mixture with cream in large bowl with electric mixer or process until combined, return to lamington pan; cover, freeze overnight. Serve sprinkled with nuts, if desired.

COCONUT CINNAMON PUFFS

¾ cup plain flour
½ cup self-raising flour
½ teaspoon ground cinnamon
½ teaspoon ground cardamom
1 teaspoon powdered saffron
340ml can coconut milk
1 tablespoon hot water
oil for deep-frying

SYRUP
½ cup water
1½ cups castor sugar
½ cup brown sugar, firmly packed
1 clove
1 cinnamon stick

■ Can be made 3 hours ahead.
■ Storage: At room temperature.
■ Freeze: Not suitable.
■ Microwave: Not suitable.

Serves 4.

1: Sift dry ingredients into bowl, gradually stir in coconut milk and water.

2: Deep-fry level tablespoons of batter in hot oil until well browned and cooked through. (The oil should not be too hot as this will brown the puffs too quickly before the centres are cooked.)

3: Add puffs to sugar syrup in pan, stir gently. Serve hot puffs sprinkled with extra coconut, if desired.
Syrup: Combine water and sugars in pan, stir over heat without boiling, until sugar is dissolved. Add clove and cinnamon stick, bring to boil, simmer, uncovered, for about 3 minutes, or until slightly thickened.

LYCHEE, GINGER AND LIME ICE

425g can lychees
2½ cups water
1½ cups castor sugar
1 teaspoon grated fresh ginger
1 large orange, segmented
1 teaspoon grated lime rind
¼ cup lime juice

- Ice can be made 3 days ahead.
- Storage: Lychees, covered, in refrigerator; ice, covered, in freezer.
- Freeze: Lychees not suitable.
- Microwave: Not suitable.

Serves 6.

1: Drain lychees, reserve syrup. Combine water, sugar and reserved syrup in pan, stir over heat, without boiling, until sugar is dissolved. Bring to boil, stir in ginger, boil, uncovered, 5 minutes.

2: Chop orange segments, stir into lychee syrup with rind and juice, simmer, uncovered, 3 minutes; cool.

3: Pour mixture into lamington pan, cover, freeze for about 2 hours or until almost firm. Transfer mixture to bowl, beat with fork, return to tray, cover, freeze until firm. Serve ice with lychees.

Bowl and spoon from Gallery Nomad

Glossary

Here are some terms, names and alternatives to help everyone understand and use our recipes perfectly.

ARROWROOT: used mostly for thickening. Cornflour can be used.

BAKING POWDER: a raising agent consisting of an alkali and an acid. It is mostly made from cream of tartar and bicarbonate of soda in the proportion of 1 level teaspoon of cream of tartar to ½ level teaspoon bicarbonate of soda. This is equivalent to 2 level teaspoons baking powder.

BAMBOO SHOOTS: the tender shoots of bamboo plants, available in cans.

Clockwise from left: Bamboo steamer, wok and wok chan, mortar and pestle and bamboo skewers.

BAMBOO SKEWERS: can be used instead of metal skewers if soaked in water overnight or for several hours to prevent burning during cooking. They are available in several different lengths.

BAMBOO STEAMER: available in various sizes, the base should be soaked in cold water for 10 minutes before using. See picture above.

BASIL: see picture top right.

BEAN SPROUTS: the sprouts used in this book are mung bean sprouts; these should be topped and tailed, available fresh or canned in brine. See picture centre right.

BEEF:

Eye fillet: tender-loin.

Minced beef: ground beef.

BLEND OR PROCESS: to "blend or process" ingredients means that a good result will be obtained by either blending or processing. However, if we just say "blend", we mean that the mixture needs

124

to be fine in texture and the processor will not do the job well enough.

Basil (top), fresh coriander.

From left: Leek, bean sprouts, red Spanish onion and green shallots.

Clockwise from bottom left: Bok choy, cabbage, Chinese cabbage, broccoli, Chinese broccoli, English spinach.

BOK CHOY: see picture above.

BREADCRUMBS:

Packaged dry: commercially packaged breadcrumbs.

Stale: use 1 or 2 day old white bread

made into crumbs by grating, blending or processing.

CALAMARI: squid.

CARDAMOM: an expensive spice with an exotic fragrance. It can be bought in pod, seed or ground form.

CHICKEN:

Breast fillets: skinless, boneless fillets cut from the breast available whole or in halves.

Thigh fillets: skinless, boneless fillets cut from the thigh.

Clockwise from top: Chopped red chillies, small (bird's eye) chillies, dried chilli flakes, chilli powder, dried red chillies and large fresh chillies.

CHILLIES: see picture above.

CINNAMON: fragrant bark used as a spice available in sticks (quills) or ground.

CLOVES: dried flower buds of a tropical tree; available whole or ground.

COCONUT: use desiccated coconut unless otherwise specified. To toast: stir coconut in pan over heat until lightly browned, remove from pan, cool.

Cream: available in cans and cartons; coconut milk can be substituted, although it is not as thick.

Flaked: coconut flesh that has been flaked and dried.

Milk: can be bought in cans but is also easy to make using desiccated coconut. (Coconut milk is not the liquid inside the mature coconut.)

Place 2 cups desiccated coconut in large bowl, cover with 2½ cups hot water, cover, stand until mixture is just warm. Mix with the hand, then strain through a fine sieve or cloth, squeezing out as much liquid as you can. This will give you about 1½ cups thick milk; it can be used when canned coconut cream is specified.

The same coconut can be used again; simply add another 2½ cups hot water, and continue as above; this will give you a watery milk. It can be combined with the first thicker milk and is a good substitute for the canned coconut milk specified in our recipes. It can be blended or processed, then strained.

Powdered milk: a substitute for coconut milk, but is not as rich as coconut cream.

Shredded: coconut flesh that has been shredded and dried.

CORIANDER: see picture with Basil.

CORNFLOUR: cornstarch.

CREAM: a light pouring cream, also known as half 'n' half.

CUMIN: available in seeds or ground.

CURRY PASTE: prepared paste available in jars in some supermarkets, delicatessens and specialty food shops.

CURRY POWDER: a convenient combination of spices in powdered form. Curry powder consists of chilli, coriander, cumin, fennel, fenugreek and turmeric in varying proportions.

EGGPLANT: aubergine.

ESSENCE: extract.

FISH SAUCE: an essential ingredient in the cooking of some South East Asian countries. It is made from the liquid drained from salted, fermented anchovies. It has a strong aroma and taste. Use sparingly until you acquire the taste.

FIVE SPICE POWDER: a pungent mixture of ground spices which includes cinnamon, cloves, fennel, star anise and Szechwan peppers.

FLOUR:

Self-raising flour: substitute plain (all-purpose) flour and baking powder in the proportion of ¾ metric cup plain flour to 2 level metric teaspoons baking powder. Sift together several times before using. If using an 8oz measuring cup, use 1 cup plain flour to 2 level teaspoons baking powder.

White plain flour: all-purpose flour.

FRESH HERBS: we have specified when to use fresh or dried herbs. We used dried (not ground) herbs in the proportion of 1:4 for fresh herbs, for example, 1 teaspoon dried herbs instead of 4 teaspoons (1 tablespoon) chopped fresh herbs.

GALANGAL: the dried root of a plant of the ginger family. It is used as a flavouring, and is either removed before serving or left uneaten. See picture top right.

GINGER: see picture top right.

Fresh, Green or Root ginger: scrape away outside skin and grate, chop or slice ginger as required. Fresh, peeled ginger can be preserved with enough dry sherry to cover; keep in jar in refrigerator; it will keep for months.

Ground: is also available but should not be substituted for fresh ginger.

Clockwise from bottom left: Chopped lemon grass, fresh ginger, fresh lemon grass, dried galangal, galangal powder.

Spring roll wrappers (left), gow gee wrappers.

GOW GEE WRAPPERS: see picture above.

GREEN SHALLOTS: also known as spring onions and scallions. See picture with Bean Sprouts.

HOI SIN SAUCE: a thick sweet Chinese barbecue sauce made from salted black beans, onions and garlic.

Dried kaffir lime leaves (left), dried lime rind.

KAFFIR LIME LEAVES: also known as citrus or lime leaves, they give a unique flavour. We used the dried variety, which are more easily available than fresh leaves. See picture below left.

KUMARA: orange sweet potato.

LAMB:

Fillet: a small tender cut found between the loin and chump.

LEEK: see picture with Bean Sprouts.

LEMON GRASS: needs to be bruised or chopped before using. It will keep in a jug of water at room temperature for several weeks; the water must be changed daily. It can be bought dried; to reconstitute, place several pieces of dried lemon grass in a bowl; cover with hot water, stand 20 minutes; drain. This amount is a substitute for 1 stem of fresh lemon grass. See picture left.

LIME RIND: see picture with Kaffir Lime Leaves

MANJO MIRIN: a sweet rice wine vinegar used for cooking.

MORTAR AND PESTLE: most mortars and pestles are made of stone, but Thais use clay mortars with wooden pestles which have been made to cope specially with small amounts of moist curry pastes and for bruising lemon grass, citrus rind, garlic and coriander root. See picture above Bamboo Skewers, which shows a stone mortar and pestle.

Clockwise from left: dried Chinese mushrooms, baby (cultivated) mushrooms, straw mushrooms.

MUSHROOMS: see picture above.

Baby: cultivated mushrooms.

Dried Chinese: unique in flavour; soak in hot water, covered, for 20 minutes, drain. Remove and discard stems, use caps as indicated in recipes.

Straw: available in cans.

OIL: use a good quality vegetable or peanut oil unless otherwise specified.

OYSTER SAUCE: a rich brown sauce made from oysters cooked in salt and soy sauce, then thickened with starches.

PAPAW: papaya.

PEANUTS: we used the roasted unsalted variety.

PEPPERS: capsicums. We used red

and green bell peppers.

PORK:

Butterfly steak: skinless, boneless mid-loin chop which has been split in half and opened out flat.

Fillets: skinless, boneless eye-fillet from the loin.

PRAWNS: (shrimp) most of the recipes in this book use green, uncooked prawns; shell and devein before use.

RED SPANISH ONION: see picture with Bean Sprouts.

RICE: There are several ways to cook rice successfully. One method is to bring a large pan of water to the boil, add the rice gradually, boil rapidly, uncovered, for about 10 minutes or until rice is just tender; drain as soon as it is tender. Serve immediately.

If cooking rice in advance, rinse the cooked rice under cold water until it is completely cold. Spread it out on flat tray covered with absorbent paper, or cloth, leave it to dry; store in refrigerator. Rice can be frozen in airtight bags or containers for up to several months.

The evaporation method of cooking rice is easy and traditional in Asian countries. Place rice in heavy-based pan, add enough cold water to cover the rice and be about 2cm above the surface of the rice. Cover the pan with a tight-fitting lid. Bring to the boil over a high heat, reduce heat to as low as possible, keep covered, cook for about 20 minutes. Remove from heat, leave covered for a few more minutes to be sure all the water has been absorbed by the rice. Rice can be cooked in a rice cooker which alters the texture and even the taste of the rice. Follow instructions with your appliance, or use the evaporation method given above as a guide. Rice is easy to keep hot in a rice cooker. Rice can be reheated, covered, in a strainer over boiling water, or in a microwave oven.

Clockwise from left: Short grain rice, jasmine rice, long grain rice.

Flour: ground rice.

Glutinous: (sweet or sticky rice) when cooked has a soft chewy texture.

Jasmine: Thai long grain rice.

Long grain: elongated grains.

Short grain: about half the length of long grain rice, but thicker.

RIND: zest.

ROCKMELON: cantaloupe.

ROSE WATER: an extract made from crushed rose petals.

SAFFRON: the most expensive of all spices, is available in threads or ground form. It is made from the dried stamens of the crocus flower.

SAMBAL OELEK: a paste made from ground chillies and salt.

SEAFOOD STICKS: made from processed Alaskan pollack flavoured with crab.

SESAME OIL: made from roasted, crushed white sesame seeds. It is always used in small quantities. Do not use for frying.

SESAME SEEDS: there are 2 types, black and white; we used the white variety in this book.

Clockwise from left: Shrimp powder, shrimp paste, dried shrimps.

SHRIMP: see picture above.

SNOW PEAS: also known as mange tout, sugar peas or Chinese peas.

SOY SAUCE: made from fermented soy beans. The light sauce is generally used with white meat, the darker variety with red meat. There is a multi-purpose salt-reduced sauce available, also Japanese soy sauce. It is a matter of personal taste which sauce you use.

SPINACH: see picture above Bok Choy.

SPRING ROLL WRAPPERS: see picture above Gow Gee Wrappers.

SQUID: a type of mollusc, also known as calamari. Cleaned squid hoods are available.

SUGAR: ordinary white granulated crystal sugar.

Brown: soft, fine, brown sugar.

Castor: fine white granulated sugar.

Palm: fine sugar from the coconut palm. It is sold in cakes, also known as gula jawa, gula melaka and jaggery. Palm sugar can be substituted with

brown or black sugar. See picture below.

Raw: natural light brown granulated sugar or "sugar in the raw".

Palm sugar.

TAMARIND SAUCE: if unavailable, soak about 30g dried tamarind in a cup of hot water, stand 10 minutes, allow to cook, squeeze pulp as dry as possible and use the flavoured water.

TOFU: made from boiled, crushed soy beans to give a type of milk, a coagulant is added, then the curds are drained and cotton tofu is the result; this is the tofu used in this book. Silken tofu is undrained and more fragile. Store tofu in the refrigerator covered with water, which must be changed daily.

TOMATO SAUCE: ketchup.

TURMERIC: a member of the ginger family, its root is ground and dried, yeilding the yellow powder which gives curry its colour; it is not hot in flavour.

Clockwise from left: Rice vermicelli, rice sticks, dried egg noodles, fresh rice noodles.

VERMICELLI: see picture above.

VINEGAR: we used both white and brown (malt) vinegar in this book.

Rice: seasoned vinegar containing sugar and salt.

WHITE FISH FILLETS: we used flake unless otherwise specified. Any white fish can be used.

WINE: we used good quality red and white wines.

WOK: see picture above Bamboo Skewers

ZUCCHINI: courgette.

Index

QUICK CONVERSION GUIDE

Wherever you live in the world, you can use our recipes with the help of our easy-to-follow conversions for all your cooking needs. These conversions are approximate only. The difference between the exact and approximate conversions of liquid and dry measures amounts to only a teaspoon or two, and will not make any noticeable difference to your cooking results.

MEASURING EQUIPMENT

The difference between measuring cups internationally is minimal within 2 or 3 teaspoons difference. (For the record, 1 Australian metric measuring cup will hold approximately 250ml.) The most accurate way of measuring dry ingredients is to weigh them. When measuring liquids use a clear glass or plastic jug with metric markings.

If you would like metric measuring cups and spoons as used in our Test Kitchen, turn to page 128 for details and order coupon.

In this book we use metric measuring cups and spoons approved by Standards Australia.

- a graduated set of 4 cups for measuring dry ingredients; the sizes are marked on the cups.
- a graduated set of 4 spoons for measuring dry and liquid ingredients; the amounts are marked on the spoons.
- 1 TEASPOON: 5ml
- 1 TABLESPOON: 20ml

NOTE: NZ, CANADA, USA AND UK ALL USE 15ml TABLESPOONS.
ALL CUP AND SPOON MEASUREMENTS ARE LEVEL.

DRY MEASURES

METRIC	IMPERIAL
15g	½oz
30g	1oz
60g	2oz
90g	3oz
125g	4oz (¼lb)
155g	5oz
185g	6oz
220g	7oz
250g	8oz (½lb)
280g	9oz
315g	10oz
345g	11oz
375g	12oz (¾lb)
410g	13oz
440g	14oz
470g	15oz
500g	16oz (1lb)
750g	24oz (1½lb)
1kg	32oz (2lb)

LIQUID MEASURES

METRIC	IMPERIAL
30ml	1 fluid oz
60ml	2 fluid oz
100ml	3 fluid oz
125ml	4 fluid oz
150ml	5 fluid oz (¼ pint/1 gill)
190ml	6 fluid oz
250ml	8 fluid oz
300ml	10 fluid oz (½ pint)
500ml	16 fluid oz
600ml	20 fluid oz (1 pint)
1000ml (1 litre)	1¾ pints

WE USE LARGE EGGS WITH AN AVERAGE WEIGHT OF 60g

HELPFUL MEASURES

METRIC	IMPERIAL
3mm	⅛in
6mm	¼in
1cm	½in
2cm	¾in
2.5cm	1in
5cm	2in
6cm	2½in
8cm	3in
10cm	4in
13cm	5in
15cm	6in
18cm	7in
20cm	8in
23cm	9in
25cm	10in
28cm	11in
30cm	12in (1ft)

HOW TO MEASURE

When using the graduated metric measuring cups, it is important to shake the dry ingredients loosely into the required cup. Do not tap the cup on the bench, or pack the ingredients into the cup unless otherwise directed. Level top of cup with knife. When using graduated metric measuring spoons, level top of spoon with knife. When measuring liquids in the jug, place jug on flat surface, check for accuracy at eye level.

OVEN TEMPERATURES

These oven temperatures are only a guide; we've given you the lower degree of heat. Always check the manufacturer's manual.

	C° (Celsius)	F° (Fahrenheit)	Gas Mark
Very slow	120	250	1
Slow	150	300	2
Moderately slow	160	325	3
Moderate	180	350	4
Moderately hot	190	375	5
Hot	200	400	6
Very hot	230	450	7